Studies on the Chinese Market Econ

China's Social Security System

Chief editors:
Gao Shangquan *and* Chi Fulin
Written by:
Sun Xiuping

FOREIGN LANGUAGES PRESS   BEIJING

First Edition 1996

The project is aided by
(Hainan) China Foundation for Reform and Development Research.

ISBN 7-119-01733-0

Published by Foreign Languages Press
24 Baiwanzhuang Road, Beijing 100037, China

Distributed by China International Book Trading Corporation
35 Chegongzhuang Xilu, Beijing 100044, China
P.O. Box 399, Beijing, China

Printed in the People's Republic of China

Editor's Note

The establishment of a socialist market economy pressingly needs the establishment of a social security system that conforms to the market economy. The establishment of a new type of social security system is the groundwork for social stability, social guarantee for the development of the market economy and a very important component part of economic structural reform, therefrom an important subject in China's marching toward a market economy. Since its founding, China Reform Development Research Institute (Hainan) has attached great importance to the study of China's reform in social security. Entrusted by UNDP and Hainan Provincial People's Government, the institute, in 1992, completed the research and study of "the reform of social security systems in Hainan and China," which won good praise from both Chinese and foreign specialists, and was publicized in authoritative foreign publications. Around the time, it also ran a series of seminars and training classes, such as "Training Class of Social Security Reform in the National Structural Reform Sector," together with the State Commission for Economic Restructuring in November 1991, the "International Seminar on Social Security and Economic Reform in China," together with UNDP, the World Bank and International Labor Organization in December 1992, and the "International Training Class on Social Security Reform in China," together with the State Commission for Economic Restructuring and the World Bank in March 1993. These activities helped promote extensively the further study of social security reform in depth and integrate it closely with reform practice.

The book is based on the above-mentioned studies, discussions, research and training classes. Many well-known Chinese and foreign specialists and scholars participated in the seminars or lectured in the training classes, contributed their valuable academic theories, thoughts and views. Particularly at the "International Seminar on Social Security and Economic Reform in China," over one hundred specialists and scholars from UNDP, the World Bank, the International Labor Organization, as well as from the United States, Japan, Australia, Switzerland, Singapore, Hong Kong and China held extensive and heated discussions. Many of the viewpoints in the book are from their essays, speeches, lectures and exchanges of views at the seminar and training classes. We express our sincere thanks to them.

The book emphasizes the current situation and major problems in China's social security reform, the systematic and penetrating exploration of ideas and models of the reform and the concrete planning of the reform. It stresses practice in the compilation. All the discussed issues came from China's practice in social security reform, and deal with the major contradiction and crucial points of the social security system in China's move toward a market economy, in an attempt to form, through the discussions, specific conceptual and operational plans that help and push forward the reform practice. The book is of a strong exploratory nature. It presents Chinese and foreign specialists' different ideas and viewpoints in discussing questions, even the intense debates and confronting viewpoints, instead of giving the sole answer and conclusion, to readers, who may compare, differentiate and draw food for thought, to acquire beneficial enlightenment from it.

Contents

Chapter I

The Present Situation and Ways of Thinking in Reforming China's Social Security System

1. The Present Situation and Problems in Reforming the Social Security System

(1) Active experiments have been made since the end of 1970s in reforming China's social security system

China's social security system was established in early 1950s for taking care of such cases as retirement, industrial injury, birth, illness and death. This system was immediately put into practice in state, joint state-private, private and cooperative enterprises if they employed more than one hundred workers. With the completion of the socialist reform drive later in that decade, and the consequent change of ownership of the enterprises, the security system went into effect in all state and joint state-private enterprises. Similar systems were also gradually established for collectively-owned enterprises in urban districts and county towns, in state institutions and government organs toward the end of 1950s. By 1991, social security systems covered more than one hundred million, or about 90 percent of the work force. The establishment and development of the systems helped maintain social stability.

Since China launched its economic reform program in late 1970s, social security systems have also undergone the following changes.

Raising the retirement pension fund from the whole society

Experiments of socializing the drawing of retirement pensions of workers and staff from state enterprises began in a number of cities in Guangdong, Jiangsu and Liaoning in 1984 and soon this practice was extended to all over the country. In 1986, raising the fund for retirement pensions for contract workers from the society began. At present, retirement pensions for workers are being raised in 99 percent of China's counties and cities. In such provinces, autonomous regions and centrally administered municipalities as Beijing, Shanghai, Fujian, Jiangxi, Jilin, Shanxi, Hebei, Sichuan, Shaanxi and Ningxia, the socialization of retirement pension fund is done on the provincial level. In such trades as the Ministry of Railways, Ministry of Posts and Telecommunications, Ministry of Water Conservancy, China Power Enterprises Association and China Construction Engineering Corporation, the same is being done for workers in state enterprises. In many places, arrangement for retirement insurance has been made for temporary workers. Under the umbrella of socialized retirement pension fund are some 70 million regular workers, contract workers and temporary workers or 95 percent of the total number of workers in state enterprises, and more than 12 million retirees, or 96 percent of the total number of retired workers from state enterprises. In 1991, more than 20 billion yuan were collected as old-age insurance fund, 17 billion yuan were paid as pensions with an accumulated old-age insurance fund of 15 billion yuan. Labor departments in more than 1,400 counties and cities practiced socialization of retirement pensions for workers in collectively-owned enterprises. In many places, old-age insurance arrangement has been made for Chinese workers working in enterprises invested in by foreign capital, workers in privately-owned enterprises and the self-employed in urban areas.

Contributing to this socialized retirement fund usually are enterprises under the Central Government, and those owned by provinces, cities and counties. The principle for raising the fund is fixing the rate according to expenditure with a slight accumulated surplus. Money going into the fund may be a certain percentage of the total wages, or a percentage of the total wages plus pensions. Workers in some cities and counties in Guangdong, Jiangxi, Fujian, Jilin, Shanxi, Sichuan and Ningxia are required to pay no more than 3 percent of their standard wages into the old-age insurance fund. For contract workers, their enterprises pay 15 percent of the total wages and the individuals pay no more than 3 percent of their standard wages as their old-age insurance fund. Paid out from this fund are regular and long-term expenditure such as retirement pensions, several kinds of stipends, including price stipends. Medical expense is not covered by this arrangement since it varies greatly among the individuals. Regulations for the socialization of the retirement fund and ways to manage it are made by labor and financial departments. Once they are approved by the local governments, they become effective as local administrative regulations. Non-profit social insurance organs under labor departments are charged with raising, managing and paying the old-age insurance fund. To this end, the Ministry of Labor has set up the Social Insurance Fund Office and labor departments in provinces, cities and counties have altogether established 2,900 social insurance organs manned by a regular staff of 27,000. In more than 1,000 cities and counties, pensions are paid out from either the bank or social insurance organs, instead of by the enterprises the retirees have previously served.

The socialization of old-age insurance has achieved obvious results, as it has basically guaranteed the livelihood of retirees, reduced the burden of enterprises in paying pensions and expenditures to their former employees and maintained the stability of the society. Whether the enterprises are running into difficulties, or have stopped production, or have gone bankrupt, or suffer from grave natural calamities, the problems do not affect the retirees, who still receive adequate and timely pensions from social insurance agencies.

Experiment of the old-age insurance system

By 1991, the total number of retired workers in China had risen to 24.33 million who are paid 56.2 billion yuan as pensions each year. These two figures are respectively 5.7 percent and 19 percent higher than the previous year. Out of the total, 18.33 million who received 46 billion yuan pensions were retired staff from state enterprises, government offices and institutions or respectively 6.3 percent and 20.2 percent more than the figures the year before.

Since the beginning of China's economic restructuring, experimental reform has been carried out in certain aspects of the old-age insurance system, including issuing stipends to offset price rises. In order to maintain the living standard of retirees, stipends began to be paid to them in 1979 when marked prices rises took place. Specifically, when prices for eight non-staple foods went up in 1979, a five-yuan-per-person stipend began to be paid every month. When meat prices rose in 1985, meat stipends began to be paid. This time, since meat prices went up by different rates in the country, no attempt was made to unify the amount of the stipend. In 1988, prices for meat, poultry products and vegetables rose again and a monthly ten-yuan stipend was issued. When rises in prices of grain and cooking oil were announced in 1991, a six-yuan monthly stipend was introduced. A five-yuan stipend was issued when grain prices changed again in 1992.

When wage reform or unified increase of wages and bonuses occur nationally, stipends are always given to the retirees. In 1986, reform measures were introduced to the wage system and consequently, a monthly stipend of 12.17 yuan was added to the pensions of retirees. In 1988, bonuses for staff in government offices and institutions were raised and this brought with it an increase of a five-yuan stipend for the retired. In 1989, universal raise of salaries took effect in the country. As a result, all pensions were raised to the next higher level and the minimum monthly pension of 30 yuan was raised to 50. When workers had their wages increased in 1992, an additional ten yuan began to be paid to retirees each month.

Though the above-mentioned measures are temporary and can hardly be maintained as an established system, they certainly have offset the effects of price rises on retired people and guaranteed them to also enjoy the result of social development. It is only natural that when people's living standards were elevated, the life of retirees improves too.

Now the experiment of individuals contributing to the old-age insurance fund. Since the establishment of the old-age insurance system in the early 1950s, the entire old-age insurance fund is provided by the government or enterprises, individuals did not have to contribute anything. During the experiment in some localities on labor contract systems in the 1980s, individuals were made to contribute to the old-age insurance fund on a trial basis. When the labor system began to be reformed in 1986, it was decided that workers under the labor contract system should pay no more than 3 percent of their monthly wages into the old-age insurance fund. This change created a problem as two different kinds of old-age insurance existed since regular workers did not have to pay for their old-age insurance. Thus, a small number of places began to experiment with the method of having regular workers contribute to the old-age insurance fund. In January 1987, when Zhaotong City, Yunnan Province, instituted socialization of old-age pensions, it became the first in the country to have workers contribute to the old-age insurance fund, a practice that was soon followed in many other counties and cities throughout the country.

The experiment of enterprises making subsidy payments to old-age insurance fund. For years, retirees entirely relied on the old-age pensions provided by the government. In the early 1980s, a method of enterprises making additional payments to the low-level old-age insurance fund made by the government came into being in Nanchong, Sichuan Province, in an effort to solve the difficulties for retirees formerly employed in small collective factories owed by street committees in the cities. The enterprises, in accordance with their own economic capability, contribute to the old-age insurance fund for workers still working, as well as those who have retired. The amount of payment they contributed could be either high or low. The Bureau of Insurance Welfare of the Ministry of Labor and Personnel immediately reviewed this practice and, on the basis of reviewing the old-age insurance reform, put forward the bill of establishing a basic national old-age insurance system. Since then, some enterprises which performed well began to experiment with paying subsidies to old-age insurance in two ways. One was to establish subsidiary old-age insurance for workers on the payroll. The No. 2 Tradi-

5

tional Chinese Pharmaceutical Works of Hangzhou, for example, pays two to ten yuan each month for its workers, who themselves pay two yuan. The Beijing Jeep Automobile Company Ltd. pays three yuan, while its workers pay six yuan a month, all of which are to be paid together with bank interest to the workers when they retire. Another way is to pay old-age insurance for the retired workers. For instance, Liaoyang Pharmaceutical Works in Liaoning Province has established a life subsidy system for retired workers.

In Nanyang of Henan Province, Qixian County of Shanxi Province and Huangzhou City of Hubei Province, most workers also have taken part in an experimental system with individual deposits. In some other places, the method of individual deposits to old-age insurance being combined with subsidiary payments by enterprises is being tried out.

All these reforms of the old-age insurance system have achieved gratifying results. *The Decision of the State Council on the Reform of Workers Old-age Insurance System* issued in June 1991 pointed out that along with economic development the system of combining payment by the government, subsidies by enterprises and individual bank deposits, should be gradually established. The old practice of the government or enterprises being solely responsible for the entire old-age insurance should be changed. Instead, old-age insurance should be shared by the government, enterprises and individual workers.

Insurance for the unemployed

In an effort to adapt to the labor system reform and promote labor contract system, the State Council promulgated in 1986 *The Provisional Regulations on Insurance for State Enterprise Workers Waiting for Job Reassignment*, thus establishing China's insurance system for unemployed workers. When unemployment insurance is not enough to cover its spending, government financial departments will provide subsidies. This fund is used mainly for unemployment relief payments, medical subsidies and production projects for self-help. At present, more than 71 million workers have taken part in the unemployment insurance plan, 400,000 unemployed workers have been provided with relief payments, 750 vocational training bases and more than 400 production bases producing for self-help have been established in the country, and 280,000 workers have found new jobs.

The founding and development of the unemployment insurance plan has not only provided a guarantee of livelihood and service for those waiting for jobs, but also created a favorable condition and environment reforming enterprises. They have also created conditions for promoting the rational flow of labor forces and laid the foundation for cultivating the labor market in China.

Reform experiment of health care plan

China established a workers' medical insurance system in the early 1950s. As the economic restructuring has been gradually carried to new depths, the drawbacks of this medical insurance system become increasingly obvious. To begin with, the free medical care plan is a heavy burden for the state and enterprises. In 1991, 22.05 billion yuan were spent to cover workers' medical expenses in the country and 18.81 billion yuan out of the total were spent for workers in state-owned enterprises. In addition, 9.45 billion yuan were spent to pay the medical bills of retired workers, and of this 7.9 billion yuan were spent on retirees from state-owned enterprises. Secondly, the rising rate of medical expenses is too fast, since the medical cost for workers in state-owned enterprises in 1991 was 10.45 times that of 1978.

The combined medical care plan of workers with major ailments. Medium- and small enterprises, especially those in commerce, catering and other service trades often are small in scale but employ a relatively a large number of staff. The limited amount of their medical care fund is not enough to pay the medical bills when their workers experience major and serious illnesses. To solve the problem, the experiment of raising a combined medical care fund to cover the expenses of major illness has proved successful and won the attention and approval of labor departments. Most of the provinces, autonomous regions and centrally administered municipalities have launched experiments in this field. Sichuan Province, for example, is trying out this new arrangement in sixty-five counties.

Whether done by trades or county- and city-wide, the fund

is maintained by a fixed amount of several yuan per month per worker taken from the after-tax profits of the enterprises. In some regions, workers themselves are required to make a contribution, usually about 0.5 yuan per month. Both the payments made by the enterprises and the contribution by workers are put into insurance institutions. The amount of medical expenses resulting from one or a series of visits to the hospital that has exceeded the prescribed sum (usually 300 yuan) is paid by the medical care fund according to the following ratio: 80 percent if the amount is between 300 and 1,000 yuan; 85 percent between 1,000 and 1,500 yuan; 90 percent between 1,500 to 2,000 yuan and 100 percent for the amount above 2,000 yuan. The amount of the bill not paid by the fund is covered by the enterprises.

One obvious result of this combined medical fund is a great reduction of the burden of enterprises. Until this arrangement was practiced, the huge medical expenses often took their toll on the bonus funds and production development funds of the enterprises. Under this arrangement, most of the medical expenses incurred when workers receive treatment for major illness are covered by the fund, individuals only have to pay a small amount and the bills for ordinary ailment. The burden of enterprises has been greatly alleviated, which is conducive to developing production and promoting the contract system. A retail store of a vegetable and non-staple food store in Tianjin paid 8,064 yuan out of its bonus fund into the combined medical care plan in 1988. One of its workers had a serious disease and was hospitalized with a medical bill of 11,291 yuan. Out of this, 9,033 yuan was covered by the combined medical care plan and 2,288 yuan, by the welfare fund of the retail store and the worker received timely treatment. Before the establishment of the combined medical care plan, workers could not receive timely treatment when their enterprises were short of health care capital, some workers could not have their bills reimbursed in good time, which has a negative effect on their lives. With this new system, all these problems are solved so that workers no longer have to worry, instead they are likely to put more enthusiasm into production. The measure is certainly conducive to social stability. By the end of 1990, a vegetable company in Beijing had established a combined medical care fund for major ailment of 358,000 yuan. During the same period, there were 314 cases of major illness and 330,000 yuan had been paid to cover medical costs.

Experiment of combined medical care plan for the retirees. During the socialization of old-age insurance, medical expenditure of the retirees has not been listed as part of old-age insurance, because such expenditures are too large to control. As a result, medical bills of retirees are still paid by their former work places. In 1985, the Shijiazhuang area in Hebei Province took the lead in experimenting with a combined health care insurance plan. Now seventy-one counties in China's fourteen provinces, autonomous regions and centrally-administered municipalities are experimenting in a similar way.

Such insurance plans cover all retirees who are under socialized old-age plans. The fund comes from their enterprises, which contribute the money according to an arrangement of a certain percentage of the total wages or a fixed sum for every retiree. The money is put into a social insurance organ, which operates the fund. One form of the combined medical care plan is unified management of the people, money and hospital. Insurance management organs in the Shijiazhuang area, Hebei Province, and Pingdingshan City, Henan Province, operate clinics whose doctors serve retired workers. Where transfers to hospitals or hospitalization is necessary, the patients need to obtain the approval of such clinics. This arrangement, which takes care of money and treatment, guarantees medical service and control of medical expenditure. In 1991, retired workers in the Shijiazhuang area spent on average 41.2 yuan per person on medical expenses, 58.5 percent less than the average of 99.26 yuan spent by those not covered by the combined medical care plan. The second form is appropriation of medical care expenditure to the enterprises according to the number of retirees by the insurance organs with balances settled at the end of the year. In some areas, retired workers have to contribute a small amount toward their medical expenses.

The combined medical care plan has guaranteed timely treatment and reduction of medical expenditure. It has also reduced the burden of enterprises, both financially and logistically. Thus the system has been well received by enterprises and retirees. Besides, 80 percent of state-owned enterprises in the country are making their own reform of the medical insurance system, mostly issuing a part of the money earmarked for medical expenditure to workers. What is not spent can be kept by the workers while the amount over what is given to the workers can be totally or partially reimbursed. In some enterprises, individuals are required to pay 10 to 30 percent of the clinical medical bills and 5 percent of the bills incurred during hospitalization. If the individuals' spending has exceeded a certain level, the rest will be reimbursed by the enterprises. These reforms conducted on the initiative of enterprises have to a certain degree imposed control on the otherwise unreasonably sharp rise of medical expenditure.

Initial steps of reforming the industrial injury insurance system

There are three main drawbacks of the existing industrial injury insurance system. The first is the low standards of payment, which leads to difficulties in the livelihood of workers who become disabled because of industrial accidents or of the relatives of those who have died on the job. Some of these workers or deceased workers' relatives some times make such a big issue that their actions affect the production and work order in the enterprises, as well as social stability. The second is the absence of an industrial injury insurance fund and socialized management. Medium-size and small enterprises, in particular, often cannot cope with industrial accidents because of their weak economy. Once a relatively serious industrial accident occurs, the enterprises cannot bear the economic losses and industrial injury insurance costs. This of course affects the production of the enterprises and making payment in fulfilling the benefits for those suffering from industrial injury. The third is the lack of scientific standard for classifying the degree of industrial injury. Now there are only two classes: those who have totally lost the ability to work, and those who have partially lost the ability to work.

Experiments of reforming the industrial injury insurance

system began in 1989 in Haikou City, Hainan Province, and Donggou County, Liaoning Province and they have been extended to more than thirty counties or cities in fifteen provinces. To push forward such a reform, the ministries of labor and public health drew up the *Standards for Appraising the Degree of Industrial Injury and Vocational Diseases*, which divided injury into ten classes. In more than 2,000 counties and cities, labor appraisal organs have been set up.

The rough framework for reforming the industrial injury insurance system in areas where experiments are being tried is expansion of coverage to bring all workers in state-owned enterprises, regular employees in enterprises with foreign investment (in some cases private businesses are included), contract workers and seasonal workers under a unified structure of industrial injury benefits and standards. Those who are totally or seriously disabled receive monthly payments for the disabled; relatives of the deceased workers are paid a monthly stipend according to the living standard where they live and one lump sum payment of 20-month standard wages. An industrial injury insurance fund is set up for long-term insurance care.

Though experiments of reform in this field have just begun, positive results are already obvious. Firstly, enterprises have been relieved of the original financial burdens. After an industrial accident took place in a factory in Haikou City, Hainan Province, the insurance agency paid all the medical bills of 16,000 yuan. The insurance that the factory had until then paid to the insurance agency was just 6,000 yuan. Secondly, the livelihood of the workers suffering from industrial injury has been ensured. When a small enterprise in a county in Liaoning went bankrupt, the insurance agency took care of making industrial injury payment to its workers. Originally, several dozen families of workers who had died of industrial accidents could not fully receive the pensions due them. Now their compensation pay is guaranteed. Thirdly, production and work order in enterprises have been guaranteed. In the past, it usually took more than a month to settle a case of industrial accident. Since the reform, however, the insurance agencies took only three days to settle the cases in two factories. Neither the injured workers nor relatives of the deceased go to factories to appeal. Fourthly, safe production in enterprises has been promoted. The practice of insurance fee is fixed according to safety norms of the enterprises as well as the punishment and bonus system based on the increase or decrease of industrial accidents make enterprises pay more attention to safe production and lowering industrial accidents.

Farmers' old-age pension experiment

China is a large agricultural country since 900 million, or 80 percent of the national population, live in rural areas. Naturally, 80 percent of the old people in China are found in rural places. For thousands of years, farmers in old age totally relied on the care of their land and families. In the past, to raise kids in order to be taken care of in old age was the basic pattern of life. Along with the reform and opening up, the role of farmers' families in taking care of the old has been greatly reduced. This is because under the impact of the commercial economy and foreign way of thinking, the traditional concept has changed. Young farmers have an increasingly weak consciousness of taking care of the old, and old people do not want to be burdens on their children. Such development is most obvious in coastal areas. Family planning has greatly changed the family structure, and gradually one young couple will have four old people and one or two children. Their financial burden will be very heavy. Moreover, the economic basis in rural areas is rather delicate, and how to take care of the old has increasingly become an urgent issue.

Along with the development of the rural economy, from the beginning of 1990s, some large and medium-size cities and their suburbs, as well as some of the rich areas along the east coast, have spontaneously established old-age farmer insurance or stipend systems with the village as the grassroots unit. According to incomplete statistics, more than 190 counties in 19 provinces, autonomous regions and centrally-administered municipalities experimented with old-age farmer insurance system and farmers in more than 8,000 villages in 800 townships were under old-age insurance schemes in 1989. Now, more than 800 counties have been approved to experiment with the old-age farmer insurance system, and out of these counties 140 are already collecting old-age insurance payments. The basic method in these experimental counties is that all farmers, whether engaged in agricultural production or township enterprises, join the unified insurance scheme with a progressive accumulation plan. The money comes mainly from individual payments with an appropriate sum of supplement from the collectives. Old-age pension is paid on a monthly basis according to the accumulated amount (including interest earned) insured. Farmers' old-age insurance offices should be set up under the civil affairs departments at the county level to be charged specifically with old-age insurance work in rural areas and operate the old-age insurance fund.

Old-age insurance plan for workers in collectively-owned enterprises offered by the People's Insurance Commpany of China

At present, according to statistics, the People's Insurance Company of China operates old-age insurance businesses only for workers in collective enterprises in more than 300 cities as well as counties and towns, because of a number of reasons. The problem with this scheme is that the coverage scope is small and only well-to-do enterprises are covered. It does not guarantee paying retirement pensions either.

(2) The primary stage in the reform of the social security system

Despite the reforms carried out in social security in recent years, the system is still at a primary stage, and faces many of the following difficulties:

Irrational mechanism

The present social security system is characterized by the state taking care of the entire cost while individual workers contribute no payment whatsoever. Such a system does not encourage the self-sponsored insurance consciousness on the part of individuals, but leads to a total reliance on the state and enterprises and induces various kinds of waste and increasing burdens for the state and enterprises to bear.

Narrow coverage

The present social security system provides coverage to those working in state organs and institutions, state-owned enterprises and some of the collective enterprises. Workers in other collective enterprises, the self-employed, Chinese workers working in enterprises with foreign investment and farmers, which together make up 70 percent of the population, have no social security coverage.

Low socialization

Apart from the old-age insurance, no insurance schemes are socialized. As for old-age insurance, by and large, it operates by a fund raising arrangement at the city and county levels in most areas in the country. All insurance management and services are basically the job of enterprises.

Incomplete system and chaotic management

Insurance items are incomplete and there is no unified planning and coordination among different insurance schemes. There is neither unified arrangement in leadership, management, operation, provision of services or supervision. Different insurance items are under the management of different departments. Even same items are still under different managements. Insurance management organs often overlap, exerting an adverse effect on efficiency and increasing the cost of insurance management.

Lack of effective operation methods for social security funds

Diversion and waste of insurance funds often occur, giving no guarantee to the increase in value of favorable balances of the funds. There is no unified amount to be put into the insurance funds by different enterprises for old-age pensions, medical care coverage, unemployment and industrial injury payment, which means the enterprises do not compete on equal terms. To have state-owned enterprises, especially large and medium-size ones, take care of all the welfare of the workers during such occasions as giving birth to children, life in retirement, being ill and death, housing and the employment of their relatives is detrimental to activating the enterprises and increasing their economic profits. In the enterprise reform focusing on the transformation of the operational mechanism and including such areas as labor, personnel and income distribution, as well as in readjusting the economic structure, improving the combination of productive elements, improving economic performance and solving fundamental contradictions in the national economy, questions of what to do with surplus officials and workers and how to bring about a rational flow of workers among different regions and enterprises will certainly arise. China also faces the problem of an aging population. It is expected that by 2000 there will be 129 million to 135 million people, or more than 10 percent of the population, above the age of 60. The solution to the question of how to ensure "provision for the elderly" must be considered right now. Along with the development of the commodity economy and the establishment of the competitive mechanism, risk factors for the laborer increase. Family planning and change of lifestyles have reduced the function of the family as an insurance factor. All these questions depend on improvement of the social security system and development of the insurance industry for solutions.

Practice has proved that reforming the social security system and establishing an adequate social security structure are prerequisites and imperative issues for the smooth progress and success of the restructuring of the economic system.

2. The Basic Principles and Overall Goals of the Reform of the Social Security System

(1) The establishment of a socialist market economic system urgently calls for the reform of the present social security system

The 14th National Conference of the Communist Party of China explicitly pointed out that the establishment of a socialist market economic order is the basic target of the reform of the economic system. This breakthrough has provided an important basis for establishing and improving a new type of social security system in China. Under the market economy, the drawbacks of China's traditional social security system have become increasingly obvious, making the reform in the system an important and urgent task.

The relationship between being just and efficient

To establish a socialist market economic system, it is imperative, among other things, to actively have a social security system covering unemployment, old age and medical care. Justice and efficiency are two basic principles of such a social security system. The relationship between the two is also a basic question that we are faced with during reforming the original and improving a new type social security system.

Establishing a social security system appropriate to the requirements of the market economy

Of the three great systems—the unified socialist market system, the urban socialized service system and the social security system, the last one must also be placed into the market and competitive context so as to increase its efficiency. China's traditional social security system is strongly characterized by a supply system on a maintenance basis which was practiced during the early years of 1950s. Its main feature is the overall responsibility of the state and management by the enterprises. Its drawback is that workers are totally dependent on the enterprises which in turn rely on the state for provision. An ultimate result is increasing burdens for the state and enterprises, making it impossible for the original social security system to continue for long. The free medical care system is one good example. During the 7th Five-Year Plan Period (1986-90), the annual increase rate of the total medical spending in the country was 23.32 percent, a figure that greatly exceeded the growth margin in state revenues and increase in public health expenditure. Though the cost of social security for the workers grew enormous and increasingly became a heavy financial burden, the lack of cost and expenditure consciousness of those enjoying the protection, and the absence of an effective control mechanism and management, resulted in the waste of limited social security resources and the failure of the system to exert the functions of encouraging those who perform better and punishing those who do otherwise. These are lessons we must draw from when considering and finalizing a new social security system. Concrete methods for encouraging frugality and reducing waste, for example, should be available as a component part of the workers' health insurance. Workers themselves may have to contribute a certain percentage to the medical insurance fund.

When visiting the hospital, they should pay a certain percentage of the medical cost.

A "safety network" and a "shock reducer"

Jiang Zemin, General Secretary of the Communist Party, pointed out in his report delivered to the 14th National Congress of the Party that while efforts are made to actively establish a socialist market economic system, develop a unified national market and further expand the role of the market, macro-control of the economic development by the state must be strengthened and improved so as to overcome and reduce the drawbacks and negative effects of the market. Social security is one of the important parts of the macro-control policies of the state. The gradual establishment of the socialist market and the competitive system, the bankruptcy and annexation of enterprises, the change of hand of property rights, all invariably bring with them risks, including the widening of the gap in income resulting from factors beyond the individual's control such as maternity leave, getting old, being sick, being handicapped, death and losing jobs. This requires a social security system, which takes into account of both being just and ensuring efficiency, so that there is a "safety network" or "shock reducer" to ensure that the market economy can operate smoothly.

Entering the market on an equal footing

From a micro- and the enterprise's point of view, the establishment of the social security system has its immediate significance. Change of the operational mechanism of the state-owned enterprises, especially, the large and medium ones, so that the enterprises can enter the market, activate themselves in their operation and raise their strength is a key link in establishing a socialist market economic system. To do so, the enterprises have to shake free of such burdens as providing all kinds of social services, including social security services, to their workers. Only when a highly unified, socialized and specialized social security system is established, can the enterprises concentrate their efforts and energy on improving production and join in the competition in the market on an equal footing.

(2) Being just and efficient: toward a new social security system

A social security system with Chinese characteristics should maintain the following principles:

The unification of responsibility, rights and interests: This means the guarantee of laborers to receive material assistance to maintain the basic need of life, when having lost the ability to work or having to stop working because of old age, being sick, suffering from industrial injury or being unemployed. This is a basic condition for ensuring social stability and economic development.

The unification of being just and efficient

Socialization. First, development of social security services should correspond with the social and economic development of a given time and the coverage and resources of funding of social security should gradually expand. Second, the management, services and supervision of social security should become socialized.

The safety, maintenance and increase in the value of social security fund. Legislation, auditing and supervision of the social security system should be strengthened.

Unified leadership and separation of the management, daily operation and administration.

Proceeding from reality. The reform and improvement of the social security system must be done on the basis of the fact that China has a large population, a poor economic background and low productivity. They must be adaptable to the requirement of the developing socialist market economic system.

The overall strategic goal for the reform of the social security system is the establishment, by the end of the century, of a new type of social security system which is appropriate to the development of the market economy, and truly guarantees the basic rights of the livelihood of the citizens, through reforms focusing on the existing unemployment, old-age and health insurance system.

—To gradually expand social security coverage, initially establish and improve a basic and unified insurance system of old age, unemployment, industrial injury, health care and birth and maternity care that is suitable to various kinds of enterprises, and create a favorable environment for changing the operational mechanism of the enterprises, readjust industrial structure and expand opening up to the outside world.

—To guarantee life and promote production. Since the guarantee of basic material needs of life for laborers under conditions when they have lost the ability of work or have to stop working because of old age, sickness, industrial injury or being unemployed is a basic condition for ensuring social stability and economic development, it is necessary for the forms, items and standards of social security coverage, the ways and methods of fund raising to be based on guaranteeing the basic needs of life. The material basis for such a guarantee must correspond with the development of productivity. In this sense, the social security system must observe the principle of being both just and efficient so that it can guarantee life and at the same time promote development of production, and be conducive to establishing a mechanism that encourages laborers' enthusiasm for work and raises the economy's efficiency.

—To establish a fund raising system with contributions from the state, enterprises and individuals, a rational mechanism for fund raising and a system supervising the effective use of the fund so as to promote the healthy development of the social security system.

—To establish a social security management system with the state making the unified legislation, governmental departments exercising unified leadership, social security organs running the operations, financial and auditing organs as well as trade union and enterprise representatives participating in supervision. In accordance with modernized social production and the requirement of a socialist market economic system, the management responsibilities of social security should be transferred from the enterprises to specialized management organs. The socialization of the management and service of social security should be strengthened, so that commodity producers are freed from the burden of taking care of specific social security operations.

—To timely establish a social security system in rural areas along with the development of the rural economy, so as to ensure stability and the implementation of the family planning policy in the countryside. Social security in rural areas should adopt different standards and take different forms in accordance with the different economic levels and trades. The standards of social security should be in conformity with the actual ability of the farmers. Funds should be based mainly on individual payment, augmented with collective contributions as an auxiliary source and supported by favorable state policies. The disposal of social relief funds and funds for helping the poor should be combined with developing production as closely as possible.

3. The Ways of Thinking for Reforming the Social Security System

(1) Reform of the old-age insurance system

The main drawback of the existing old-age insurance system lies in the separation of the spending and the raising of the fund, i.e., the separation of the rights and obligations. For quite a number of years, the raising from the society of the old-age insurance fund did play a positive role in balancing the enterprises' burden of taking care of the retired and promoting social stability. This practice, however, has a strong tendency of total equalitarianism, making it impossible for the three major sectors of the old-age insurance system, the insurers, the enterprises and old-age insurance management organs to combine their interests and mutually check each other. This results in the absence of an inner motive force in the system which has to be maintained by administrative measures. This is the main reason why the present system runs into more and more difficulties, and also a main question that has to be solved through reform.

A comparison of China's experience in the past forty years in insurance for the old and the practice of other countries in the last hundred years reveals three different goals of choice in reforming China's present system: one is to reform and perfect the present practice of raising old-age insurance funds from the whole society, expanding the range of fund raising and coverage of the insurance, increasing the percentage of funds raised from the society, adding new items for fund raising, and improve and perfect fund raising methods; the second is to gradually move over to compulsory individual account deposits for old-age insurance; and the third is to proceed from China's reality and learn the strong points of both fund raising from the society and individual account systems to create a new type of old-age insurance system that is suited to the development of a socialist market economic structure.

Making adjustments to the present old-age insurance system is relatively easy and can keep the system running in the short term. The lack of checking and control mechanism in the system, however, makes it impossible to scientifically handle the relationship of development and aging of the population and will run into more problems with the increase of the burdens carried over by older generations. To insist on adjusting such a system will not only hinder the introduction of reforms but also leave more obstacles for future reforms.

A gradual move to individual deposit accounts, a system with relatively high efficiency and a stimulant mechanism, will avoid the crisis of making unprepared payments at the height of the aging of the population and social problems brought by older generations.

The already existing burdens of taking care of retirees and the inability of enterprises and workers to shoulder both burdens of putting money into the combined socially raised fund and making advance payments toward individual accounts will invariably lead to conflict between the designed total accumulative fund system and the actual partial accumulative fund system.

Thus, the reform of China's old-age insurance system must take immediate and long-term interests into consideration. On the one hand, the strong point of the present system in having the whole society contributing to the insurance fund must be preserved and perfected while its shortcoming of total equalitarianism—"or everybody eating from the same big pot"—must be overcome. The self-guarantee mechanism of the individual deposit account system should be introduced while its lack of a social assistance nature should be avoided. Eventually, a new, socialized, scientific and systemized old-age insurance order, which combines the strong points of both Chinese and foreign, traditional and reformed systems, social and individual's own initiatives, is both just and efficient and unifies both rights and obligations, will be established.

Through reforms, the present single-level old-age insurance fund raising should give way to a multi-level system that combines both the basic and additional insurance, so as to meet the different requirements of the insurer.

In fund raising for old-age insurance, it is projected that the present practice of making payment only when it is needed will be replaced by one that combines both social mutual aid and making advance payment through compulsory deposits; the system of total fulfillment by the state and enterprises will be replaced by combined efforts jointly by the state, enterprises (the employer) and the individuals. Enterprises will be the main contributors of the basic insurance fund while individuals will be the secondary contributors. The sum to be contributed by the individuals should be low at the beginning and they should gradually shoulder up their total responsibility along with their wage increases, rise in income and their economic strength. The additional insurance funds will consist of both the enterprise and individual additional insurance, both of which will adopt the individual public accumulation account system. The sum of enterprise additional insurance can at the present stage be decided by enterprises according to their performance. When conditions ripen, laws should be adopted to set levels for enterprise additional insurance. Individual additional insurance shall be linked with the basic insurance and forced deposits are required to gradually go from a low to a high level.

In managing the old-age insurance fund, a system combining a mutual aid old-age fund and an individual old-age fund will take the place of the current unified raising and spending system. Funds from different sources will be put into different accounts, and operation of such funds will be highly public so as to increase the confidence of the insurer. The basic insurance fund will be under the social mutual aid fund account under the ownership of all insurers. The additional insurance fund will be listed under workers individual old-age fund account under the ownership of the specified individuals. The use of the social mutual aid fund and individual old-age fund shall be governed by old-age insurance laws and management orders established according to such laws. All insurers will have their individual old-age accounts, and have a fixed numbering system which will never change and be accessible throughout the country, listing in detail the revenue, payment, bank interest, withdrawal and transfer of insurance relations of the insurer. Great efforts will be made to realize the socialization and modernization of the management of old-age insurance system.

In paying out old-age insurance fund, payment from the combined basic and additional insurance funds will replace the present pension payment. The system of linking the paying of insurance fund with the contribution of the insurance fund will replace the present system of paying pensions according to certain payment standards that the retiree meets. The paying of the basic insurance fund will be based on the percentage that workers have contributed out of their wages. The duration of contributing to the insurance fund will decide the amount of pay they receive. Funds accumulated under the individual deposit accounts will be transferred to an additional insurance fund to be paid out monthly throughout the life of the insurer after he or she retires from work, calculated according to average life span. In case the insurer decides to live in another country or dies, all the fund, both the principal and interest, under his or her account, will be paid out at one lump sum to the insurer or his or her immediate relatives.

In order to realize a smooth transition from the old to the new insurance system, and gradually reduce the burden brought by succeeding of generations, insurers under different insurance systems may enjoy different ways of receiving old-age insurance pay, such as new insurers getting paid according to the new system, the insurers under the transit system, according to the transit system and the old, the old system. "Old insurers" here refer to those who retired before the introduction of the reform and they will continue to be covered according to the State Council's (1978) No. 104 Document. "New insurers" refer to contract workers, temporary workers and those who begin to work after the implementation of the reform. All these new insurers will enjoy the new old-age insurance benefits. "Transit insurers" refer to workers already under employment when the reform is implemented and who, therefore, can choose between the two systems on the principle of enjoying the most advantageous arrangement of the two.

Reform of the old-age insurance system is a social project that will change the benefit distribution relationships of several generations. For the individual worker, old-age insurance means guarantee of a balanced life-long consumption. For the society, it means making sure that the funds raised in the manner of insurance will, on condition of satisfying the basic need in the life of the old-aged, realize a balanced revenue and expenditure at all times. Before any decision is made, careful forecasts and study of the reform plans must be undertaken so as to make the reform plan rational, practical and scientific. Through scientific studies, the ratio of the old-age insurance fund raised and accumulated must be in conformity with the economic development level, population development reality, and the ability to endure on the part of the state, enterprises and individual insurers. Besides, it is important for the old-age insurance fund to have a favorable balance so as to avoid a paying crisis during the height of aging of the Chinese population.

(2) Reform of the health care insurance system

The existing health care system has the following major problems:

Lack of a control mechanism of health care expenditure, and serious waste of medical resources. To be brief, the present health care system in China is one of "the patient receiving treatment, the doctor writing the prescription and the state (enterprises) paying the bill," a system that encourages sharp rises in expenditure and tremendous waste.

Lack of sharing of the sickness burdens and increasing burden on the state and enterprises. Since the enterprises are solely responsible for paying medical expenses, those who have a small staff, and are economically poor, often can only provide funds for ordinary illness treatment and do not have the financial resources to take care of workers seriously or critically ill. Thus, for some workers there is no guarantee of receiving medical care.

Absence of effective management and supervision of health care service and the existence of many loopholes. In recent years, some hospitals have adopted the management mechanism as enterprises and this has induced a tendency of pursuing nothing but economic profit. Some doctors prescribe unnecessarily expensive medicine for their relatives or friends, and some even try to peddle ineffective but very expensive medicine in order to obtain kickbacks. The result is a sharp rise of health care expenditures.

Then what should be the way out for the reform of the health care insurance system?

It should be borne in mind that China is a large country with many ethnic groups, an expansive landmass, a huge population, uneven development in the economy, and a modern industrial society co-existing together with a traditional agricultural society. This fact has mandated that it is inappropriate for China to have one unified social security system. All the provinces, autonomous regions and centrally administered municipalities should be encouraged to establish a social security system adaptable to their own conditions and a social security mechanism that has many levels and in different forms.

It is necessary, however, to have a unified basic principle for a multi-level social and economic security system different in form. Under the condition that this basic principle is observed, the provinces, autonomous regions and municipalities may establish their own appropriate health care insurance systems.

The basic principles for reforming China's health care system are: equality of all workers working in different economic sectors, in enterprises of different trades and under different employment terms; rational sharing of the medical expenses between the state, enterprises and individuals; guaranteed basic medical treatment for workers, reduction of waste of medical resources and a sound system of medical service and insurance; coordinated reform of the health care insurance system with the reform of medical service units and the medical market structure.

Health care insurance funds should come from the enterprises (the employer) and workers themselves with the former paying the most part and the individuals contributing a sum that is economically bearable. It is not necessary to set a unified standard of payment since conditions in different localities as well as health care levels vary.

Management of medical expenses should be strengthened. Coverage of health care insurance should be based on actual need and not be too extensive. Normally, serious ailment should mainly be covered so as to increase the individual's awareness of expenditure and at the same time guaranteeing basic treatment for those seriously ill.

Special health care insurance organs should be established to exercise unified management. Effective supervision, examination and checking mechanisms over the medical and pharmaceutical units and their supply channels should be established. Administrative, economic and legal measures should be adopted to deal with those elements in the medical and pharmaceutical trade and medical service units that hinder the reform of the medical care system so as to ensure the smooth progress of the reform.

Laws on health care insurance should be drafted and adopted. Like insurance in any other areas, the operation of health care insurance depends on law. The rights and obligations of social security management organs, medical service units, enterprises and workers should be clearly defined so that the health care insurance system is legally effective and operates within the framework of law.

Reform of the free medical care system should be in step with that in health care insurance for enterprise workers and the medical service so that the gap between the two should not be two big, in order to avoid the medical care consumption moving toward the higher end.

The sharp rise in medical expenditure and waste of medical resources must be held in check. While efforts are made to increase the individual workers' awareness of medical care cost, efforts must also be made to control and deal with hospitals and the pharmaceutical industry.

The policy of putting prevention first must be adhered to. Support should be give to encourage people to engage in exercise to improve their physical condition and reduce illness occurrence, which is conducive to improvement of the public health and reduction of medical cost. It is, therefore, necessary to find a health care insurance method that is established on the combination of prevention and treatment.

(3) Reform of the unemployment and industrial injury insurance system

Under present circumstances, reform of the unemployment and industrial injury insurance should follow these principles: (A) Guaranteeing the basic life of laborers during the period of income cut-off, which is a basic condition for life sustaining for the laborers. Industrial injury insurance should not only guarantee the basic life for laborers after they have lost the ability to work, or have to stop working temporarily or have their work ability reduced because of industrial injury, but also should be in the interest of continuous improvement of working conditions for laborers; (B) Unity of rights and obligations. What is reimbursed is linked with what is insured in an effort to overcome total equalitarianism; and (C) Unity of fairness and efficiency. Insurance against unemployment and industrial injury should guarantee the basic life for the unemployed and injured workers, and be in the interest of promoting the competition and rational flow of the labor force, and raise labor productivity and safety in production. Unemployment insurance, in particular, should become a means of helping the unemployed find jobs as soon as possible and a motive force and guarantee for employment training, job finding and the maturity and perfection of the labor market as well as economic development.

27

The expansion of insurance against unemployment and industrial injury should bring under its coverage all workers in all kinds of enterprises and those cultural and governmental institutions that are run like enterprises, broaden the scope of those eligible for unemployment benefits, raise the socialization level of unemployment and industrial injury insurance and strengthen risk resistance ability.

To raise the fund for insurance against unemployment and industrial injury, the principle to be followed should be "making charges according to the amount of expenses with a slight surplus" so as to charge a reasonable fee. At present, the unemployment insurance fee is paid by the employer, but the individual deposit insurance should be introduced at a later date in order to raise the ability of risk resistance. Insurance fees against industrial injury should be borne entirely by the employer, and the rate should be set according to the frequency of injuries in different types of enterprises.

In paying out insurance against unemployment, the represent twenty-four-month eligible period should be shortened to twelve months, so as to reduce the cost of insuring against unemployment and encourage the unemployed to actively seek reemployment. A limit to the period for the unemployed to receive insurance payment should be set, and the length of this period should be linked with the number of years insured. The standard rate of payment should be based on the average monthly wage during the year before becoming unemployed. To those who have permanently and completely lost the ability to work, a monthly stipend should be paid. For all other cases, a lump sum payment of insurance against industrial injury should be made.

Management of insurance against unemployment and industrial injury should be improved. The basic responsibilities of managing this insurance job should be further clearly defined. Apart from daily routine work, job training, job introduction, to engage in production to help sustain oneself and service to the unemployed should be done well. Those working in the field of insurance against industrial injury should do a good job in ensuring safe production in enterprises and finding jobs for the disabled resulting from injury, in addition to defining industrial injury and making payments for the insurer. Management of unemployment and industrial injury should become more socialized in order to further reduce the social burden carried by enterprises.

Labor appraisal committees at various levels should be established and perfected so as to draw up unified and scientific standards for appraising the degrees of inability to work. In doing so, the present practice of heavily relying on what surgical injuries one can see with the naked eye, and overlooking internal injuries one cannot see with the naked eye, should be overcome.

(4) Some suggestions on the policies concerning the reform of the social security system

Socialization, an essential characteristics of social security and objective demand of the development of the socialist market economy

Gradual socialization of various insurance services will be conducive to establishing a socialist market economic system, increasing the ability of socialist security for enduring and reducing risks and promoting competition on an equal footing among different types of enterprises and the rational flow of the labor force. To this end, boundaries separating different trades, enterprises with different ownerships and workers employed under different systems should be broken down, for unified rates of charges for insurance, unified amount of basic payment and unified methods and management. Enterprises and institutions (including banks, the Peoples' Insurance Company, post offices, railway services and harbors) under the Central Government, various ministries of the government and the military shall no longer follow the practice of "having the enterprises providing insurance services." Instead, they shall all take part in the local social security system, in order to facilitate the establishment and development of a unified market system, including the labor service market.

Economic guarantee is the core for social security.

The degree of social security at any given place is ultimately decided by its economic development level and subject to the status quo in its population development.

China is a large developing country, whose society is composed of both modern industrial and traditional agricultural sectors. The economic development and population structure vary a great deal among different provinces and regions. It is therefore neither necessary nor desirable to try to establish, in the immediate future, a unified or even mono-social security model. Nor shall we try to seek fund raising in a much broader way or even throughout the country. Instead, provinces and cities should be encouraged to proceed from their local conditions to explore and establish a multi-level and varied-form social security system that is conducive to development of the market economy and long-term stability of the society, under a unified principle. At the same time, attention should be paid to coordinate between the old and new systems, the domestic and foreign systems, as well as within the social system in different parts of the country, in order to facilitate the shaping of the unified national market system, the rational flow of the labor force and the development of reform and opening to the outside world. This will also help the smooth transfer from the old to the new system and the stability and unity in the society.

Reform of the social security system should be conducted according to the economic capability of the country and the practical conditions at all places.

The reform of the social security system of any given region should conform to the objective demand of its social and economic development; the social security level should conform to the economic development level; the rate of insurance payment should conform to revenues, profit level of the enterprises and the economic condition and degree of acceptance psychologically among the individuals and the accumulation of social security fund should conform to the availability of capital, as well as the business management ability. At the beginning of reform, the rate of accumulation may be low but should be adjusted along with the increase in economic results and improvement of business management levels. To guarantee smooth reform of the social security system, the reform plan should try to minimize the cost for the transfer from the old to the new system, on the basis of careful planning.

The social security system should be built on and enforced by laws and regulations so that all social security operations will be systemized and normalized.

First, laws and regulations should be adopted to standardize rights and obligations between the social security organs of the state and society, enterprises on one part and the individuals on the other; the determination and adjustment of the rates to be paid toward and received from all insurance items; the establishment, size, duties, responsibilities and working procedures of all social security control organs; the rate to be drawn, the area and method of expending of social security administrative fees, etc. The basic law concerning social security should be made and promulgated by the state. The provinces can draw up their implementation procedures of the social security system according to the basic law and their own local conditions. All social security actions should be conducted strictly according to law; limitations resulting from deviations, willful acts and purely administrative acts should be minimized and the kind of payment from insurance coverage in the form of favoritism should be avoided. All members of the society are equal and have the same dignity in taking part in the social security system. The authority of social security should also be strengthened.

Second, it should be clarified by law the ownership of the property rights of the social security fund, namely the ownership of all social security funds belong to all those under social security coverage; the ownership of individual insurance funds belong to the individual insurers. On such basis, the three bodies in the social security system, i.e., the individuals, enterprises and administrative organs, as well as their rights and obligations, should be organically combined to form a relationship of mutually dependent and mutually conditioned, in order to promote the self-motivated and healthy operation of the social security system. The paying in and out of the insurance fee should be strictly tied to each other. The amount of fees paid, and the length of time of such payments by all insurers (including all enterprises), will directly determine the level and the period of insurance coverage, so that insurance coverage payments will truly reflect the contribution of the insurer during the period of coverage.

Changing the present system of adjusting retirement benefits by government appointing enterprises (or social security administrative organs) to one in which old-age insurance is tied to the existing wage levels of the society.

This is to say a certain percentage (80 percent, for example) of the increase rate of the average wage level in the society of the previous year is taken as the standard for the increase in the basic old-age insurance payment for the retirees, to solve the problem of low income for those who have retired in the past. Regions that practice this tie-up system shall no longer implement the regulations concerning paying subsidies and regularly adjusting retirement benefits for retirees.

China's insurance market, which is in its early stage, remains to be cultivated and developed.

Both social security and commercial insurance have a great future. Under the market economy, both should seek common grounds and complement each other. Apart from expanding and developing social security organs, the role of people's insurance companies should be maximized and they should be encouraged to take over some of the social security businesses according to the reform plan of the social security system, so that a social security system in multi-levels and in varied forms shall be created for providing increasingly perfect social security coverage for workers.

For more than a decade and particularly in the past few years, private businesses in urban areas have experienced great development. Initial statistics suggest that nationally there are 25 million people who own private businesses. Though these people have increased incomes, they also have worries in the face of market risks and, therefore, are deeply interested in taking part in social security schemes. In light of this new development, concrete measures should be drawn up so as to bring them into the social security system, under the principle of paying insurance fee as enterprises and individuals.

(5) Reform of the social security administrative system

The present administrative system for social security in China is no longer suitable for the reform of the social security system, due mainly to the following reasons: First, departmentalism and lack of coordination neither answer the socialization demand in sharing the risks, nor help raise administrative efficiency and reduce administrative costs. Second, the governments, institutions and enterprises do more or less the same kind of jobs in social security schemes. The indirect macro-management and direct micro-management are not separated from each other. The judicial, supervising and operational functions are mixed together, and the lack of a supervising mechanism has left many loopholes and made it difficult to determine and strengthen management responsibilities. This way it is impossible to improve management levels. Third, the scale and quality of the management organs are not suitable for implementing the reform plan. The conflict of interests between various departments and contradictions in the management system have become major obstacles for deepening the reform of the social security system. To reform the present management system and establish a new one which is scientific, rational, efficient and capable for fulfilling its management function, and can carry out the reform measures and which can adjust and improve itself, is an imperative task at present.

The socialization of production calls for the socialization of social security schemes which in turn calls for the socialization of the management. Socialization as an essential characteristics of the social security system is both an important target for the reform and the inner demand of the management of the system.

To realize socialization of social security management, the following principles should be observed; the principle of unified socialized management toward different economic elements, different categories of enterprises, workers under different economic systems, and of retirement, medical care, unemployment and industrial injury coverage; the principle of separating the governments, institutions and enterprises from each other in the management organizational setup, separating indirect macro-management from direct micro-management, and separating judicial, supervisory and operational organizations from each other; and the principle of combining management with services (including community management and service) and combining economic insurance with service insurance (including labor service, facility service and information and consulting services).

The multiple levels of the society and the social security system have decided the multi-level nature of the management of social security schemes. The organizational setup and the functions of social security management can be divided into the following three levels.

Macro-management level

Social security committees of the state and provinces should be set up as governmental organs for the management of social security and exercise of governmental social security functions and being responsible for the coordination of the judicial, supervisory and planning departments, as well as the drawing and revision of various social security reform plans. An efficient office should be established as the permanent organ charged with the daily routine work.

Such government organs responsible for labor, public health, civil affairs, personnel, planning, finance, auditing and supervising should all exercise necessary administrative supervision on social security institutional and management organs.

Social security fund committees on old-age, medical care, unemployment and industrial injury should be set up as representatives of the main bodies of the social security schemes such as the government, enterprises and insurers for the supervision of the revenue, expenditure, management and investment of all social security funds.

The implementing level

Social security bureaus should be set up at the city and provincial levels which are, under the leadership of the government (through social security committees), responsible for the operations of various social security undertakings, including the collection and management of insurance fees, payment of insurance benefits, efficient capital guarantee and service guarantee for the insurer institutions and individuals.

Micro-operational level

Social security bureaus and grassroots social security offices should be set up and charged with the operations of social security matters. They shall collect and make payment from insurance fees as well as community services. The grassroots offices can also run social security and monetary deposit businesses within the area under their responsibility, so as to promote the local financial development with insurance and support insurance with monetary businesses.

The management of social security funds is a major aspect of social security management. Whether social security funds are run well and whether they are efficiently used or whether the preservation and increase of their value is maintained on a long-term basis are determining factors for the success of the social security system. According to statistics made by the Ministry of Finance, in 1991, 24.409 billion yuan of old-age insurance fees was collected from state-owned enterprises by labor departments throughout the country. During the same period, 20.2 billion yuan was spent (out of the total, 18.85 billion yuan was paid to veteran retirees) with a favorable balance that year at 9.209 billion yuan and an accumulated favorable balance of 14.627 billion yuan. Apart from some 3 billion yuan that was spent on buying government bonds, the rest was put in the bank. In addition, 5.084 billion yuan was collected as old-age insurance from collectively-owned enterprises. During the year, 4.538 billion yuan was spent (direct expenditure was 4.332 billion yuan) leaving behind a saving of 0.546 billion yuan for the year and a accumulated saving of 1.808 billion yuan. Some 0.837 billion yuan toward unemployment insurance fund was collected and 0.25 billion yuan was spent (out of the total expenditure, 24 million yuan went to the unemployed as relief help). That year's saving was 0.587 billion yuan, with an accumulated sum of 2.518 billion yuan. Under present conditions, to put social security funds in the bank or to buy government bonds will not realize the goal of increasing the value or preserving the value. Along with implementation of accumulated old-age insurance system, the preservation and increase of the social security fund will become more severe.

Experiences in China and abroad have shown that the preservation and increase of the value of social security funds can only be realized through combining insurance with monetary undertakings. This means, in accordance with the principle of combining safety with efficiency, social security funds should be invested in projects that are low in risks, highly efficient and conducive to local economic development, through indirect and multi-direction investment. To this end, it is necessary to establish an investment operational organ for social security funds according to the principle of separating government, institutions and enterprises from each other. First, an insurance bank may be established and people well-versed in insurance and financial matters should be put in charge of investment businesses with insurance funds. Second, a specialized bank or non-banking financial organization may be entrusted with investment businesses with insurance funds. The organization should be paid a commission or management fee or a certain percentage of the profit in a manner of contracted service. Third, a social bank may be set up with certain stock shares contributed by insurance investment. No matter which form the investment operational organization may take, social security funds should enjoy full autonomy in investment operations in accordance with the separation from social security committees and social security bureaus as in the case of separating the government, institutions and enterprises from each other. At the same time, the investment operation should accept the supervision of the social security committees and bureaus as well as the social security fund committees. Steps must be quickened in drawing up the management responsibilities and methods, targets, principles, directions, channels and division of interests, risk obligations in investment businesses and the management supervision procedures, so that every conduct will have rules and regulations to follow, all malpractice with social security funds for private benefits will be blocked and the safety of social security funds will be ensured. Governments should offer support to investment operations with social security funds in information direction, favorable policies, project priorities and financial guarantees.

Necessary supervision on the operational process and organizations of social security undertakings is an effective measure for ensuring healthy development of social security undertakings, as well as respect for the citizen's rights of the insurant. Whether social security supervision is carried out completely and effectively, is an important indication of the degree of maturity of the social security system.

The establishment and improvement of various kinds of supervision organizations are preconditions for carrying out supervision on social security undertakings. Such supervision includes that by the state power organs—people's congresses at various levels and their standing committees when the full congresses are not in session, the administrative supervision by the governments (through their various departments), judicial supervision by the judicial organs, inner supervision of the social security organs and the democratic supervision by the people. All such supervision should have established organs, staff, system and regulations, and be really responsible instead of existing only in name.

To make social security management better known, realize the openness and democratization of social security management and establish a mechanism for insurers to have the opportunity to take part in supervising are the keys for doing the supervisory job well. All implementation procedures of the social security system, the functions and responsibilities of social security organs and their working procedures, should be clearly standardized and made publicly known, for the examination and supervision of the people at any time. All insurers have the right to question the management organs and be told about the insurance fund and the total accumulated sums they have contributed, as well as what they are receiving as insurance payment.

4. Reform Plans and Practices: Hainan, Shenzhen, Xiamen and Nanchang

(1) The reform of social security system in Hainan Province

Basic ways

In early 1989, the State Council made Hainan Province one of the experimental places for reforming the social security system. Giving full attention to this task, the provincial government in Hainan set up a leading group and an office under it for the provincial reform of the social security system. In more than two years, the leading group did a great deal of investigation and research into the history and existing situation of social security in the province and comparative studies on the social security system in Hainan and those in other Chinese provinces and foreign countries. On this basis, the provincial government put forward its overall tentative plan for reforming the social security system in Hainan Province, as well as five specific reform plans on workers' retirement pension, unemployment, industrial injuries, health care and free medical care systems. Then the provincial government conducted comprehensive, qualitative and quantitative simulation calculation and forecasts, as well as a series of discussions and debates participated by specialists from China and abroad on the overall tentative plan and the specific plans. In 1991, the province twice sent people to report to eight organs in the Central Government. Opinions from workers and residents in the province were also heard on an extensive basis. Having gone through several revisions, the reform plans were finally released by orders of the provincial government in late 1991. At the same time, a provincial social security committee and a social security bureau under the provincial government were set up. The plans became effective as of January 1, 1992 among all workers in the enterprises in the province.

The basic way of thinking and the projection of the plans

(A) Reform of the social security system must proceed from the subjective demand of the development of the market economy and the need of adapting to the economic construction in the special economic zone.

First, the barriers between various economic sectors and enterprises such as the state-owned, collectively-owned, privately-owned and those owned by foreign capital were broken down. Thus the principles of unified rates, unified starting point of payment, unified methods and unified management were adopted so that all kinds of enterprises are entirely equal as far as the social security system is concerned. This changed the situation of different burdens for different enterprises and promoted enterprise competition on an equal footing.

Second, the differences of treatment between managerial staff and ordinary but regular workers and further those differences among regular workers, contract workers and temporary workers were abolished. All workers, so long as they take part in social security coverage according to regulations and pay the required fees, would enjoy the provisions of the system. In other words, everybody performs the same kind of obligation and enjoys the same kind of rights, no matter what specific job he or she does. Thus, not only all enterprises are equal, all workers are equal under the social security system.

(B) The standards of the social security system must be appropriate to economic development and population growth in the province. The existing payment for the social security system was considered too high and the burden for the insurer was too heavy and during the reform payment should be lowered. Yet, social security management departments felt that the rate of payment was too low and could not pay for the demand of the increasing coverage. They demanded increases in contributions. One of the first issues to be solved in the reform, therefore, was to design the right level of insurance.

Placing the social security question into the overall social system, departments concerned in Hainan carried out all-round studies and repeated forecasts of the history, future development and their interrelations of the economy, population and social security in the province. They also invited the N0. 710 Research Institute of the Ministry of Aeronautics and Space to make comprehensive and concentrated simulation and forecast research on the development of the economy, population and social security in the coming sixty years in the province, by combining the efforts of designing staff and professional forecast staff and using the combined method of qualitative and quantitative analysis.

(C) Combining compulsory and mechanical methods

Instead of the past practice of heavily relying on administrative measures, departments in Hainan persisted in the methods of adopting laws and working within the legal frame to implement the security system, so that social security operations became systemized, standardized, man-made obstacles and deviations were reduced or avoided, irregularities and limitations associated with administrative measures were overcome. At the same time, the combination of legally enforcing the social security system and the mechanism of the system itself has rendered inner motivations for sound operations of the social security system.

In this regard, the existing retirement pension system is a good example. In the past, paying of retirement pensions was not related to paying for social security coverage. Thus, the rights and obligations of the workers were separated from each other. As a result, to pay less or delay paying contributions to social security schemes always occurred even though management departments worked hard and adopted many compulsory measures to enforce payment. The major reason for this was the absence of a mutually conditioning mechanism among the workers, enterprises and social security management departments. During the reform in Hainan, experiences from abroad were learned and a new type of retirement social security scheme was established which linked up the payment for and receiving of social security coverage and unified the rights and obligations. Instead of issuing simple retirement pensions, the practice of combining basic old-age insurance payment and additional old-age insurance payment and linking up the issuing of basic old-age insurance payment with the insurer making the basic insurance contribution was adopted. Specifically, an average salary converted on the basis of an index figure of the number of years that a worker has worked is considered the basic old-age insurance payment, so that this basic payment really reflects the contributions the worker has made during his working life and the entire basic old-age insurance fee he has contributed and becomes a delayed payment for his work during his working lifetime. During his working years, payment as additional old-age insurance contribution is directly put into the worker's personal account. After his retirement, the principal and interests are made available to him as additional old-age insurance. As a result, the amount of insurance fee paid by workers and their enterprises and the length of such payment directly decide the level of old-age insurance coverage benefits workers receive after their retirement. The mechanisms of unifying rights and obligations has promoted insurers' awareness of self-protection in safeguarding what they should receive for their work, and thus urges enterprises and insurers to pay the full amount of insurance fees and do so in good time as well as supervise insurance management organs to improve their job so as to guarantee the normal, stable and effective operations of old-age social security system.

(D) Social security system must be socialized, systemized and scientific.

First, the situation of multiple management had to be changed and a unified and socialized provincial management system was established so as to strengthen the capability of resisting and dispersing risks, lower management costs, improve management efficiency, promote the synchronized transfer of the functions of enterprises and the government and transform social security undertakings as enterprise behavior into truly social behavior.

Second, all social security systems were brought under the framework of laws so that the behavior of the three main sectors, i.e., the insurer, the enterprise and the management organ, were standardized, in order to facilitate the defining of management responsibilities, improving management skills and guaranteeing the honest contact of management organs and personnel.

Further, proceeding from scientific management principles, administrative organs and government institutions, administrative organs and enterprises, the supervision organs and actual operation organs as well as indirect macro-management functions and direct micro-management functions were separated from each other, in the setup of management organs. A unified, multi-level structural management system with an inner supervision mechanism was established, including the following levels:

Macro-leadership level. A provincial leading body for social security undertakings—the provincial social security committee was set up to be in charge of law enforcement, supervision, coordination of tasks and design of all kinds of reform plans for social security undertakings in the province. Labor, health, civil affairs, finance and auditing departments are responsible for their own administrative supervision tasks as part of their functions.

Intermediary management level. A provincial social security bureau was set up as the actual operation organ for all social security undertakings, and was charged with the management of revenue and expenditure of social security funds. At the same time, social security funds committees for retirement pension, health, unemployment and industrial injury consisting of representatives from the government, enterprises, workers and social security specialists were also established to supervise the operations of the revenue and expenditure of social security funds.

Micro-executive level. City and county social security bureaus and grassroots social security offices were established to specifically conduct the collecting of social security fees and making social security payments. Social security offices were set up according to the layout of enterprises and insurers and might be in charge of monetary deposit and social security businesses within their jurisdiction at the same time.

(E) Operation, protection and increase of the value of social security funds: insurance and monetary deposits were combined out of consideration for security and benefits. It is difficult to protect and increase the value of social security funds if they are simply put into the bank or used to buy bonds. Successful experiences from abroad were learned, and it was decided to take the road of combining monetary and insurance businesses. The government in Hainan has had three kinds of plans: one is to establish a provincial insurance bank; another is to organize local development banks by selling shares; and the third is to entrust the job to several non-banking monetary organs. Under the supervision of the provincial social security committee and social security bureaus and various special social security fund committees, social security funds are invested, through indirect and multiple direction investment, into low-risk projects that have relatively good returns and are conducive to the development of the economy of the province, so as to guarantee the protection and increase of values of social security funds, according to the principle of combining security with benefit. To this end, the government provides necessary support to the operation of social security funds in such areas as information orientation, favorable policies, priority in projects and financial guarantees. It is possible to combine the reform in social security system with that in the housing system, by putting the accumulated social security funds into the construction of housing and allowing and encouraging workers to build housing with their accounts of personal social security fund (such as up front payment or installment). This way, not only the two problems that exist in the present housing reform, i.e., shortage of funding for building houses on the part of the government and shortage of funds for buying houses on the part of workers, are solved, but also the protection and increase of value of social security funds are guaranteed.

The effect of the new social security system and the idea for the future

Since its introduction in January 1992, the new social security system in Hainan Province has been doing well. Practice proves that the reform of the social security system in Hainan has made quick progress, as it is an improvement on the old system both in scope and depth.

It has widened coverage and increased socialization. There are items covered by the new social security system, including old-age, unemployment, industrial injury and health insurance. There are now more people covered by the system, as workers in enterprises of all kinds of ownership in the province and workers in all government institutions that are practicing an enterprise management system are all participants of the social security system, making it a system for the society as a whole.

It has effectively guaranteed the basic rights for life for the retired, disabled and unemployed and thus promoted social stability. Up to now, more than 85,000 retirees, over 40 workers suffering from industrial injury and more than 130 unemployed workers have received funds for basic living according to regulations and in good time. As a result, "the old are taken care of, the sick are treated and the unemployed get relief."

It has strengthened the insurance mechanism and raised the social security contribution rate. The combination of making insurance contributions and making insurance coverage payments, the unification of rights and obligations and the overall consideration of fairness and efficiency have had a great impact on workers and enterprises for timely paying insurance contributions, promoted strengthening of management by management organs and made the new system effective and stable since its introduction.

It has reduced the social burden of some enterprises and promoted competition of various types of enterprises on an equal footing. The new system unified the rates of social security charges and payment base, exempted retirees from paying obligations and thus reduced the burden of some old enterprises. According to statistics, in the first half of 1993, 476 enterprises had their social security payments reduced for a total sum of 9.9928 million yuan.

Besides, the implementation of the new social security system in Hainan has greatly pushed forward enterprise reform and promoted the development and deepening of reform in labor, wage, housing and personnel systems.

(2) The reform of social security system in Shenzhen City

In 1989, the State Commission of Economic Restructuring made Shenzhen City and Hainan Province experimental zones for reforming the social security system, providing the deepening of reform in these areas with an invaluable opportunity. Shenzhen City spent three years on investigating, studying, consulting and learning from the experiences of the social security system in developed countries, giving birth to the comprehensive concept of combining the reform of the old-age retirement pension system, workers health care system and linking up such reform with workers housing reform, assistance of the society and self-protection. The "Provisional Regulations Concerning Social Security in Shenzhen City," which the People's Government of Shenzhen City declared on May 1, 1992 for implementation on August 1 was drafted on the basis of this idea. The proclamation and implementation of this comprehensive reform plan that linked up old-age insurance, health care insurance and public accumulation fund for housing (insurance against industrial injury and unemployment remained unchanged.) indicated that social security undertakings in Shenzhen took a new step forward.

Main features

(A) To combine old-age, health care and housing insurance into a package deal promotes the most efficient use of limited resources.

Old-age insurance, health care and housing were the three "most difficult issues" that had long troubled Shenzhen City. To solve them one by one would waste resources and create contradictions between them. The reform this time fully made use of their differences in the timing for requiring funding so that the limited funding resources could be most efficiently used.

(B) Further expanding coverage for old people

To adapt to the need of various economic elements, the "Provisional Regulations" extended the coverage for the old people to all kinds of enterprises of various elements, government institutions that are run as enterprises and workers of neighborhood committees (except workers from foreign countries, Hong Kong, Macao and Taiwan) in Shenzhen. Since its introduction, all workers, no matter what position they hold, or the nature of their work place, so long as they and their work places pay old-age insurance fees, will enjoy the appropriate insurance fund and coverage after they retire. This is conducive to realizing equal pay for equal work for workers.

(C) In management, old-age insurance fees come from the public accumulation fund and individual's personal account.

Social security institutions set up the old-age insurance public accumulation fund as well as the individuals' personal insurance account, the last of which is more closely tied to the obligation of paying the insurance fee with enjoying insurance coverage payments, thus establishing a mechanism of encouraging people to work hard, make more contributions, save more funds and receive more coverage. This measure has also more closely linked up the interests of workers with the economic performance of their enterprises so as to increase the adhesion of the enterprises.

(D) Replacing the labor protection health care and free medical care systems with workers health care insurance system

Specifically, on one hand, funding for health care is drawn from the society and people in the system mutually help each other. Through the drawing of public funds, money formerly under the disposal of all units themselves is put together into a workers' health care insurance fund which ensures that all workers enjoy health care, laying aside their worries, fully bringing into play their enthusiasm for work and make them concentrate without worry on their jobs. On the other hand, the fund is managed in a unified way, so as to encourage frugality and reduce unreasonable expenses. As a result, the burden of health care on all units is reduced, fund saving and waste reduction measures are adopted. For example, a worker has to pay 10 percent of the medical bills when the expenses exceed a certain fixed amount. When the excessive part is so high that it goes beyond a prescribed limit, the worker does not have to pay the additional excessive part.

(E) The public housing fund system

According to the "Provisional Regulations," enterprises are obliged to pay 13 percent of the total wages of their workers into the public housing fund. The implementation of this system will gradually change distribution of housing among workers from distribution in kind to distribution of money. This means adjustment of the relationships between the enterprises and workers in two areas: for the enterprises, instead of shouldering the task of providing housing for their workers, they will increasingly offer compensation to their workers, depending on the length and degree of contribution. The longer one has served, the greater contributions one has made, the more public housing funds he will receive. For workers, in order to receive more public housing funds and enjoy the guarantee for housing, to work hard and make more accumulation is the basic way out while at the same time, paying more attention to the economic performance in the enterprise.

Another feature of the public housing fund system is its link with the old-age retirement coverage fund. Once the "Provisional Regulations" has been implemented and savings in the individual's personal account and the personal account in the public housing fund have accumulated, workers, when buying housing space, can borrow part of the money in the old-age retirement fund and pay it back to the public housing fund later.

(F) Adjusting management organs and clarifying responsibilities

Social security organs are established according to the principle of separating law enforcement and supervision from execution. Under the Shenzhen People's Government, there is a social security committee in charge of evaluating and revising social security regulations, coordinating policies related to social security schemes, deciding on the operation of large sums of social security funds and reviewing and supervising social security operations. Under leadership of this committee is the social security administration, which is charged with running old-age insurance, public housing fund and industrial injury insurance business. There is also the health care insurance administration charged with running health care insurance work. While it is under the leadership of the city's social security committee, the daily work of the health care insurance administration falls under the leadership of the city's health bureau. This new type of social security administrative system is conducive to the development of social security undertakings and puts social security work under the unified planning and leadership of the government, creating favorable conditions for implementing the comprehensive social security reform plan.

(3) The reform of social security system in Xiamen City

The comprehensive social security reform plan in Xiamen City has the following features:

Unified insurance system, expanded coverage

In Xiamen City, major changes were made to correct the chaotic situation in which enterprises owned by the state, collectives and those with foreign investment and even in the same enterprises, regularly hired workers, contract workers and managerial staff followed different social security arrangements. As a result, all legally registered economic entities in Xiamen, including those owned by the state, collectives, private individuals or with foreign investment are regarded as equals and all the Chinese workers and managerial staff hired by these enterprises are on an equal footing. And they are all under the same system, whether it is old-age pension system, unemployment insurance, medical care arrangement or industrial injury insurance.

Modified ways of raising, managing money and paying money in social security schemes

(A) Reforming the ways of raising money

First, enterprises now pay the due amount as one lump sum. In the past, various insurance items and even the same kind of insurance were managed by different institutions, enterprises had to pay the amount separately in several sums. Now as they only pay once, the enterprises' workload has been reduced.

Secondly, index standards for paying social security fees have been set. Take the old-age pension for example. It was decided that enterprises pay 15 to 21 percent of their total wages and individuals pay 3 to 8 percent of their wages. Then what are the standards for the different rates between those figures? It is not the nature of the enterprises nor the position of individual workers. The decisive factor is the reasonable common features between them: the ratio between the monthly wages of a given enterprise (or a worker) and the average monthly wages in the city. Obviously this ratio reflects the economic position of a given enterprise or a worker in the society and the economic ability to endure the charges. Besides, whether you pay more or less, it all goes into your own account which is closely related to what you are going to receive in the future, thus it is a reasonable arrangement.

Thirdly, all individual workers make contributions to old-age insurance schemes. In the past, only some of the workers pay a certain percentage of money into old-age insurance no matter what their ability to endure was. Now all workers pay a certain amount according to the index standards, marking a visible progress.

Fourthly, most of the payment for old-age insurance goes into individual accounts. After the reform of the system was introduced, it was decided that there would be individual accounts as well as social accounts for old-age insurance. Of the old-age insurance contributions made by enterprises and individuals, 4 percent goes into the social account and the rest goes into individual accounts. The essence of this practice is not to divide enterprise' money among individuals, but for the sake of management of the accounts and making payments in the future. One can imagine, under the arrangement of collecting money and then paying it out instantly, workers seem to have no individual accounts and money saved, but they will receive old-age pensions without one cent less when they retire. The present practice brings with it a mechanism that greatly enhances workers' enthusiasm of taking part in old-age insurance, supervising their enterprises to make timely payments, doing away with the idea of everybody receiving the same amount despite of varied contributions, gradually unifying the rights and obligations, encouraging and accelerating the transition from the system of pay-as-you-go to the budget system based on accumulation.

Fifthly, the nature of the social accounts. The social accounts that come in as a result of reform not only have the function of paying old-age pensions to retired workers but also serves as a method for government macro-economic control as well as a kind of accumulation. To adjust such an account can adjust the time limit for the transition from pay-as-you-go to budget based on accumulation and adjust the level of old-age pensions.

Sixthly, the industrial injury insurance standards. Enterprises, as they differ in trade, pay 0.2 percent to 2.5 percent of their total wages for industrial injury insurance.

(B) Reforming the management of insurance funds

It is designed such that the social security fund is divided into social account and individual account of old-age insurance fund, unemployment insurance fund, medical care insurance fund and industrial injury insurance fund. All the funds are raised in a unified way and placed under unified management by social security organs. Social security funds should be used to make safe and profitable investments. Interest and other income of such funds should be settled once every year and transferred as principal. This way, funds formerly scattered among different insurance management organs are put together, increasing safety and facilitating supervision.

(C) Reforming the contributing and paying methods

Xiamen City made sweeping changes in the ways of charging and paying money for unemployment insurance, medical care insurance and industrial injury insurance. The idea was to reduce waste on the condition of satisfying necessary safety demands. Changes to the charging and paying of old-age insurance was more drastic. Basically the changes include the following:

Firstly, newly retired workers receive monthly old-age pensions based on the amount in the individual's old-age insurance account, average lifespan and interest rates.

Secondly, in order to guarantee basic living standards of retired workers, the government sets up minimum old-age pension rates to be paid to the workers till death.

Thirdly, the amount of old-age pension above the average wage level in the society is paid by an accumulative deduction method, so as to avoid old-age pensions going up too high above the wage level of workers still on the job.

Fourthly, newly retired workers receive retirement pensions calculated on the basis of combining different rates of retirement payments and individual accounts.

Fifthly, workers that have already retired are to receive the original treatment they enjoyed.

Reforming social security management system

The government of Xiamen City set up a social security commission to exercise leadership in policy and supervision. Original social security organs in the city were reorganized or new ones set up to be in charge of daily operations. Originally existing social security organs, as a result, were either merged or became subsidiaries and agent institutions. Agencies related to residential financial deposits were encouraged to set up.

Supervision of social security operations comes from three sources. One is the city's social security commission. The second is from the Communist Party, government and financial organs. And the third comes from social supervision committees, which consist of representatives of insurers.

Operations of social security accumulation fund

The absence of explicit regulations on the increased value of social security fund operations in Xiamen resulted in the devaluation and loss of funds. To change the situation, Xiamen City now has the following five regulations.

First, it is explicitly stipulated that "social security accumulation fund belongs to all insurers taking part in social security arrangement, not any departments or individuals."

Second, it is stipulated that the city social security commission is to decide the ways, channels, amount and division of profits of the operation of social security accumulation fund.

Third, it is stipulated that operation of the social security accumulation fund may be entrusted to concerned financial departments and investment organs. Such entrusted operations should produce returns. The government cannot directly get involved in such operations.

Fourth, when conditions ripen, a social security bank should be established.

Fifth, the increased value from operations of the social security accumulation fund should be transferred as principal.

(4) Explorations in basic old-age pension plans in Nanchang

On August 12, Nanchang City publicized the "Experimental Methods for Paying Basic Old-Age Pensions to Enterprise Workers," which marked an initial step of reform. Since then, gratifying results have been achieved.

New method for paying basic old-age pensions

According to the new method, basic old-age pensions are made up of two parts: social old-age pensions and individually-paid old-age pensions. The first part means paying out 25 percent of the monthly average wages based on the figure of the previous year in the province. The second part means 1.5 percent of the monthly wages based on the old-age insurance fee a worker has paid during his years on the job. This part closely links up the amount of insurance fees workers pay during their active working years with what they are going to receive after retirement. The formula is like this:

Basic old-age pension=monthly average wage in the society X 25% + individual's monthly wage X number of years of paying insurance fees X 1.5% + various kinds of subsidies.

The new method also offers favorable policy treatment to those engaged in special jobs and model workers. The basic old-age pension goes up, effective as of July 1 every year, by 60 percent of the average wage increase over the previous year in the province. When the average wage in the province shows no increase over the previous year, the basic old-age pension remains the same without a raise or cut. This system allows sharing of the economic development in the society by retired workers.

The scientific feature and feasibility of the new method

(A) To adapt to the demand of the socialist market economy

The new method has an obvious positive role in adapting to and developing a market economy and transformation of the mechanism of enterprises. To begin with, it guarantees the basic need of workers in retirement, thus greatly reducing the friction of interests and instable factors that may lead to social upheavals that have been brought about by the reform. Secondly, it visibly promotes social productivity and competition among enterprises, workers, their qualities and contribution. Finally, it overcomes the irrational phenomenon of the previous old-age pension system, turning social security from an enterprise to a social behavior, avoiding overburden on enterprises and creating an equal and favorable environment for enterprises to take part in market competitions so as to adapt themselves to the subjective demand of the socialist market economy.

(B) To adapt to the demand of reforming three systems

The new method satisfies the demand of reforming three systems. First, a major reason affecting the flow of the labor force among enterprises of different ownerships is the deficiency in the social security mechanism. The existence of different social positions for workers as they work in enterprises of different ownerships has led to the traditional thinking that "small collective enterprises are inferior to big collective enterprises, which in turn are inferior to state owned enterprises." Under the new method, the total number of years of paying insurance contributions overcomes the drawback of the previous method which did not allow workers to add up the total number of years they have worked if they have worked in enterprises of different ownerships. The new method, which applies to all workers, no matter they are shop floor workers or managers, regular workers or contract workers, state-owned factory or non-state owned factory workers, so long as they pay the insurance fee, thus reforming people's employment concept and promoting employment reform. Second, the old method took the standard wages as the basis for calculation, separating the linking between retirement pension and the type of work workers engaged in. Standard wages were only part of the original wages, excluding job subsidies and bonus or overtime pay. To take such standard wages as the basis made the retirement fee unreasonable, affecting adversely the living standard of retirees, forcing enterprises and workers to seek elevation of grades and limiting the roles of bonus and other forms of distribution. Along with reform of the wage system, enterprises can now decide their own wage distribution, overshadowing the importance of standard wages. To pay workers only with standard wages means a big margin reduction of their income and less guarantee for their living standard. The new method takes the total income as the basis, thus overcoming the drawbacks listed above and satisfying the demand of the reform of the wage system. Third, the new method is particularly applicable to workers engaged in very hard, dirty, tiring and high risk jobs. Workers on the shop floor in these jobs usually have high pay when they are young and active. This means their pension has a high index, a practice that will have an encouraging effect for them and all other workers. The principle of those who make more during their working years will receive higher pensions in retirement is conducive to mobilizing workers and helps activate income distribution within enterprises.

(C) Taking structural old-age pension as the basis

The new method divides the old-age pension into two major parts: One is called the social old-age pension, which is paid on the basis of 25 percent of the average wages in the province in the previous year, in addition to various kinds of subsidies. This part is meant to satisfy the basic need in the life of retired workers. The second part, called old-age pension based on insurance contributions, is based on the average wage of the individual worker. According to the number of years he has made insurance fee payments, it is divided into three classes. For every year he has made payments, he will receive an additional pension payment of 1.5 percent, 1.3 percent or 1.1 percent. This is to link up his labor, contributions and insurance fee payments with his pension. Compared with the old method, which based his pension on the standard wage of the last month before his retirement, this better reflects his service results. The old method made stair-like jumps of increases, which is not reasonable. The new method practices a certain percent of increase for every one more year of paying insurance fees. Such an increase is smooth and reasonable. Besides, when the number of years is made a factor deciding the level of pensions, it really guarantees that the number of years of service decides the level of pensions. As the new method links up the basic old-age pension with the wages out of which a worker pays insurance fees, the number of years he makes such payments and his contributions, it has enhanced workers' consciousness in taking part in the social security arrangement.

(D) Establishing an adjustment mechanism

Compared with the old method, the new method has the characteristics of having a normal adjustment mechanism. In the absence of a normal adjustment mechanism under the old system, old-age pensions had no link with the rise of wages and inflation in the society, so retirees could not share the development of the economy. As a result, the real income of retirees dropped. The new method has done well in dealing with the relationships in two aspects. One is the relationship between economic development and the current retirement system. Owing to historical reasons, the present pension for retired workers is low, as it is fixed on the basis of the standard wages workers received just before their retirement. Further once fixed, the amount of the pension did not go up. Old-age pensions neither had any close links with the quality and quantity of the workers performance during their active working years, nor could they increase along with the development of the economy and the improvement of people's living standards. The consequence was that the state had to "patch things up" by issuing various kinds of subsidies and stipends to offset the drop of living standard for workers. The other is the relationship between guaranteeing life in retirement and production development and social stability. Retirees have worked hard during their working years for the economic development of their enterprises and social progress. What they dread most is that they are neglected and forgotten by the society once they have retired. The reform of the old-age pension system thus has two tasks: really guaranteeing the worker's life making them feel that they are moving forward with the society and time, so as to promote social stability and progress. The new method has established an adjustment system, stipulating that old-age pensions increase, as effective on July 1 every year, at a rate of 60 percent of the previous's total average wage increase in the society in the province. When there is no such increase in the general wages, no adjustment to the pension shall be made. This practice guarantees that retired workers share economic development.

(E) Following the principle of combining fairness and efficiency, rights and obligations

First, the relationship between being fair and efficient. The new method pays attention to dealing well the relationship between being fair and efficient, so that the new system better guarantees life. Structurally speaking, social old-age pensions are paid on the basis of 25 percent of the average monthly wages in the province in the previous year. This means that in 1992, each retiree received a monthly pension calculated on the basis of 25 percent of the monthly average wage in the province in 1991 (38.38 yuan out of 153.3 yuan). This figure, plus subsidies and stipends, gave each retiree at least 89.38 yuan. This same sum was paid to everyone whether economic returns in the enterprises they belonged to was good or bad, since the idea here is to reflect the principle of equality in social security arrangement. The part of old-age pensions based on the insurance contributions paid by individuals allows the retiree to receive 1.5 percent for every year he has paid the fee. This reasonably reflects the differences based on the periods of services workers have made. To link up their pensions with their services during their working years reflects the principle of economic efficiency. Along with the development of the economy, workers still active on the job receive increased wages, because they have directly created the economic results. The retirees receive 60 percent of the increased amount, because they have retired and been absent from direct production. They did, however, make their contribution to the development of their enterprises and social progress. Thus, for workers in retirement to receive 60 percent of the increase of wages in the society reflects the principle of being fair and efficient.

Second, the relationship between obligations and rights. Social security takes the precondition of workers performing the obligation of making contributions and enjoying their rights. To link up the raising and paying out of old-age pension funds means the relationship between rights and obligations. Only those who have performed their obligations have the right to receive pensions. In the past, the state and enterprises paid for old-age pensions so that even though they have received years of old-age pensions, workers did not know their rights and obligations. The result was that they had no concern for insurance undertakings and lacked the self-consciousness of taking part in insurance plans. The relationship of rights and obligations, therefore, was an important issue of the reform. Now to pay workers a certain percentage of the insurance fees they have contributed fully reflects their rights and obligations.

(F) The purpose is to guarantee the rights of the retirees

The purpose of reforming the old-age pension system and for that matter the entire old-age insurance system is to improve the life of retired workers and protect their interests. The level of the pension after the reform, therefore, should be higher than the current level, according to the Ministry of Labor. The new method is the best picked out by computers from a series of measures, on the basis of the specific conditions in the city of Nanchang, large quantities of data and investigations, and comparisons and analysis of more than one hundred reform plans different in form, content and ratios. Estimated results show, that among the 3,662 workers who retired according to the new method in 1992, 82.5 percent had increased income, specifically, they together received an increased basic old-age pension of 48,800 yuan a month, with an increase rate of 6.54 percent. The 17.5 percent whose retirement income was lower than their former income were paid basic old-age pensions. The total rise in income was 7.66 percent. The control of the higher margin took into consideration the economic strength of insurance organs and enterprises, and also fully considered the acceptability of the workers and protected their real interests.

The implementation of the new method provides guarantee for choosing one's job, as it broke loose from the limitations on the status of workers in enterprises of different ownerships. It also encourages enterprises to try their best to increase their economic efficiency, increase the wages of workers and actively make insurance contributions in an effort to protect the interests of their workers in retirement.

Since the new old-age care scheme is closely associated with the interests of every person concerned, it will encourage workers to actively contribute to the insurance fund and the society, and help them supervise enterprises to make their payments, promoting enterprises to improve their economic performance. This way, the problem of enterprises operating on contract management delaying their payments or paying short of the due amount will be overcome and workers will really enjoy the benefit of the reform.

The new method operates on a mechanism of making adjustments every year which allows retired workers to fully enjoy the fruits of economic development of the whole society, is conducive to raising the living standard of retired workers, reducing adverse effect on the life of retired workers brought about by increases in wages, inflation and currency devaluation. After all, these are the purposes of reforming the basic old-age pension system.

Problems to be solved

(A) The adjustment mechanism. The foundation for the adjustment mechanism designed in Nanchang in increasing old-age pension every July 1 by raising the pension on the basis of 60 percent of the average monthly wage increases in the previous year in the province is "average monthly social wage." Some people believe adjustments really should be based on "general index of retail prices." Others hold the view that it should be based on the life expenses and increase level of the living standard of the workers still working. The average monthly social wage on which the new method is based in comparison is more direct. And the figures from the data publicized by the provincial statistics institution are more accurate and convenient. Psychologically, these figures are more acceptable to workers.

(B) In order to maintain the continuity of policies, the new method offers 5 to 15 percent more old-age insurance funds for workers who have been honored as national or provincial model workers. One basis for this is that they have made outstanding contributions to their enterprises and the society during their working years, and it is only natural that they receive better treatment. Another reason is that during the reform of the old-age pension system, trade unions in Nanchang voiced strong opinions, demanding that former model workers should receive more benefits.

(C) According to the new method, those engaged in underground work in places such as mines, or in jobs involving work in high temperatures, will receive 0.3 percent of the average monthly wage as additional pension for every full year they have paid their insurance fee. Those engaged in jobs harmful to their health will receive 0.6 percent of the average monthly wage as additional old-age pension. Some people have pointed out that those engaged in very hard jobs may ask for and be allowed to retire early, upon examination by insurance institutions and approval by labor departments. The early retirement should not take place more than five years before the due retirement age. The Labor Bureau of Nanchang City upheld this opinion. Since workers engaged in such jobs usually have higher wages, their retirement benefits are also high.

(D) The Labor Bureau of Nanchang holds that along with the change of enterprise operation system and the reform of wages, favorable policies in issuing wages should be given to workers working on the shop floor, especially those doing hard, dirty and tiring jobs. As the gap between their wages and the income of office workers keeps widening, there is the question of whether office workers are paid reasonably. As a result of the reform, office workers' workload will increase. What now they receive and what they will receive once they have retired is simply not reasonable, inducing irrationality in the enumeration issue of the new system. The wage system needs further reform so as to rationally solve the payment problem between manual and mental workers.

Chapter II
China's Old-Age Insurance System

1. The Overall Reform Plan

(1) In 1991, the state made public regulations for reforming the old-age insurance system. Departments concerned put forward proposals for such a reform, taking an important step in developing China's social security schemes.

Since the introduction of the reform of the economic structure in China in 1978, fundamental changes have been made in implementing China's workers old-age insurance system. In the past, enterprises paid retirement expenses for their retirees, resulting in varied burdens for the enterprises. Such burdens, however, did not really have any adverse effect, since what they could not pay was picked up by the state in the form of subsidies. Things became different when enterprise reform began, since enterprises were requested to become independent and separate from the state financial budget. As a result, a scheme must be found for paying workers retirement expenses beyond the framework of enterprises. A main method is to raise funds from among the enterprises. The labor contract system, which was initially established in 1976, replaced the fixed laborer system and began the process of workers having to pay insurance funds themselves. Besides, temporary subsidies have been paid to retired workers in order to offset the effect of inflation or those caused by major adjustments of prices and wages.

According to recent statistics, during 1990 and 1991, the population of retired workers in urban areas rose by 5.7 percent to become 24.33 million. Retirement expense went up by 19 percent to 56.2 billion yuan. This was a result of not including in the wages various kinds of welfare subsidies paid to the workers in kind (such as housing).

Some people are worried that the present old-age insurance system in urban China is over-generous and therefore cannot last long. Viewed from the fact that the population is aging quickly, such worries are not groundless.

Now China has nearly 100 million people above 60 years in age, making up 9 percent of the total population in the country. The figure is expected to be 130 million in the year 2000, which will be more than 10 percent of the national population, and reach the standard for judging a population for being "old." All forecasts suggest that in the coming 40 years, the old-age population in China will increase at the rate of 3 percent annually, much higher than the total population growth rate of 1.68 percent. The percent of old people in the national population will be respectively 20.42 percent in 2030 and 21.33 percent in 2050. The rate of increase of old people in China is much higher than the average world level, including that in Europe and North America. A UN forecast says that during 1950 and 2000, the population of old people in the world will rise by 176 percent and that in China by 217 percent. By 2025, 19.8 percent of the Chinese will be old people, 6.1 percent more than the world old-age people ratio of 13.7 percent. The quick rise in the old-age people in the Chinese population will inevitably increase the spending of the state on the old people. The ratio of the old people to be provided for in China in 1964 was 11.37 percent and in 1982, 12.99 percent. This is expected to go up to 15.97 percent in 2000 and 34.79 percent in 2030.

On September 26, 1991, the State Council promulgated the *Decision on Reforming Enterprise Workers Old-Age Insurance System*, listing regulations on reforming the old-age insurance system for state-owned enterprise workers and providing guidance for developing a new old-age insurance system to replace the then existing practices. This was a significant step in developing China's social security schemes. The Ministry of Labor drew very detailed plans for implementing the decision of the State Council, which included the following:

All urban workers, including self-employed workers, regardless of the manner in which they are employed and the nature of their employers, should take part in the nationally unified old-age insurance system, which is to consist of three levels:

The first level is designed to provide basic old-age pensions for all retired workers. The basic old-age pension is to be borne by the state, enterprise and workers themselves. The standard for raising the fund and level of the pension are calculated on the basis of the total wages with a ceiling attached. The contributions from enterprises and individual workers are exempt from income tax. The old-age fund consists of two parts: one is a certain percentage of the average social wages and the other a certain percentage of the index figure of the average wages of workers during lifetime which is associated with the length of their employment. The old-age pension is adjustable at fixed periods of time so as to offset the impact of inflation.

The second level is to provide an additional old-age pension, which is drawn from the after-tax profits of the enterprises. Enterprises can, in accordance with their economic might, change the amount of the additional old-age pension. The additional old-age pension provided by the enterprises will be deposited into workers' individual accounts and upon workers' retirement, the accumulated sum, including both the principal and interest in the individual's account, will either be turned over to the workers or be transferred into life-long annual payments.

The third level is deposit-type old-age insurance that workers may voluntarily take part in. Upon retirement, the accumulated amount, including the principal and interest in workers' individual accounts, will be issued as a lump sum to the workers.

Like today, the retirement age at the beginning is to be maintained at 60 for men and 55 for women. Once the pressure on employment lessens, the retirement age may be postponed. The basic old-age insurance is implemented at the provincial level and eventually may be carried out at the national level. This scheme is to be placed under the management of non-profit administrations under the leadership of labor departments at various levels. These same administrations shall also be charged with managing the second-level insurance funds. At the third level, workers may choose their own management organs, which can be state or privately owned.

Specialists abroad have made appraisals of the reform plan by the labor department and come up with the following opinions:

(A) About the scope of coverage

The reform plan's call for establishing a nationally unified old-age insurance scheme for all urban workers is an admirable goal which once reached will make up the inadequacies in the coverage as seen in the present system, guarantee equal treatment for all urban workers and is conducive to the flow of the labor force. The plan also wishes to establish a rural old-age insurance system, which will be a step of great historic significance in China's social security development.

(B) About the old-age benefit

Compared with the present existing system, the old-age benefits in the reformed system will have the following major features:

—The single-level system is replaced by a three-level system;

—The method of fixing old-age benefits has replaced the method of combining fixing old-age benefits with fixed allocation of contributions.

Like the case of labor insurance, the first level, or the basic old-age insurance, fixes old-age benefits. The second and third levels mean fixing of allocation of contributions. Old-age benefits are decided by the accumulated amount in the individuals' account book and the accumulated amount in turn is determined by the sum put into the account and the interests it generates. If a worker is disabled or dead at an early age, and thus experiences a short period of employment, the accumulated amount will be small.

The reform plan makes no explicit regulation in regard to the subsidies to be issued for disabled or dead workers. According to the present old-age insurance system, only totally disabled workers can receive subsidies and the deceased are issued with one lump sum pension. The method suggested in the reform plan is similar to the present practice. The Social Security Convention (No. 102) of the World Labor Organization stipulates that pensions should be given regularly to the survivors of deceased workers who are covered by an insurance system. The common practice in other countries is to "borrow" part or entire potential period of service so that a pension of practical significance may be issued if a worker is disabled or dies at an early age. A pension is issued to surviving families in case workers die during their employment or in retirement. The sum of the pension is decided by the real pension of the dead or injury or disabled pension for the potential period of service which is issued to the surviving families (usually the widow/widower and orphans).

The first-level old-age insurance fund consists of two parts: one part is related to the average social wages and the other to the length of employment of the workers and the life-long average wage index. The basis for both parts is total wages. The formula for calculating the new old-age insurance clearly includes a basic part which is not related to the qualifications of individual workers, and an additional part which is directly related to the qualifications of workers. To move from taking the final wage as the basis to taking the life-long average wage index as the basis reduces the practice of giving workers a last-minute wage raise in order to increase their old-age pension.

(C) About fund raising

Under the present retirement insurance practice, almost the entire insurance fund is drawn from the enterprises. Sometimes, workers themselves contribute a sum mostly at about 3 percent of their standard wages, which is only required for workers employed by contracts. The reform plan explicitly points out that the first-level fund is to be contributed by the state, enterprise and individual workers, while the second-level is paid by the enterprises and the third by workers themselves. To draw contributions from three quarters for the basic old-age insurance fund is in keeping with practices in many other countries. Under the social security system, all three sides, the state, the enterprise and individuals, should accept obligations and bear risks.

A basic policy for the reform plan is to draw funds uniformly throughout the country. In fact, social security schemes in other countries, without exception, are nationally unified. It is thus only natural for China to unify the system in the country. Until now, however, China is the only country where recently fund raising for social security schemes starts from the grassroots (enterprises). This practice, with a very few exceptions, has not gone beyond the county (or small city) level. What prevents unified fund raising in a much broader region is the rules at each locality. There is no reason for having regularly long-term employed workers to take part in coverage different from that for workers employed by contracts. All the provinces should as soon as possible uplift the insurance coverage at the provincial level. There are possibly the following factors that hinder the breakdown of provincial boundaries in implementing a nationally unified insurance scheme: provincial differences in the ratio (of retired workers to those still on the job) and particularly in financial ratio (of old-age fund to total wages), imbalance in economic development and worries that reserve funds generated by a certain region may not be used to invest in developing that region. The basic policies and the advantages of unifying the scheme nationally should be made known to all people and necessary guarantees provided to diminish people's worries.

It is estimated that the old-age insurance funds raised by following the principle of collecting money according to expenses will increase from 17 percent in 1992 to 36 percent in 2050. Raising the entire fund is not a desirable method, not only because it immediately demands high allocation of contributions, but also inevitably accumulates large reserve funds. A method of raising part of the fund may be designed. In initial years, the percentage of contribution allocation may be set at a point slightly higher than that for fund allocations, based on expenses and in later years, the fund allocation percentage should be slightly lower than allocations based on expenses. There may be other methods for raising money. One measure is called "phased insurance fund raising method," according to which the fund allocation percentage is not adjusted every year but over a fairly long period of time. The fund allocation percentage of a given phase may be decided according to the following standard: the reserve fund must keep increasing so as to prevent reduction of the reserve by expenses, or the reserve fund should not be lower than a certain number of times over the annual expense. A multitude of fund raising methods should be designed for selecting one that is most suitable for the economic and social conditions.

(D) About investing the reserve fund

The second- and third-level insurance schemes will inevitably generate reserve funds which should be invested properly. Whether the first-level will generate any and how much it will generate is determined by the fund raising method adopted. The main standards for investing the old-age insurance fund are safety rate and profit margins. If the reserve fund keeps rising, the liquidity will not be a precondition for making the investment. Nominal returns should be higher than the inflation rate. In the case of the first-level, it should be higher than fluctuations of wages, since the first-level old-age insurance fund is related to wages. In fact, whether it is possible to find suitable and adequate investment opportunities is also a factor for choosing the method for raising the fund. At present, old-age insurance funds are mainly deposited in banks or used to buy national bonds, with a nominal annual interest rate of 5-7 percent, which is lower than the rate of inflation.

(E) About management

Management of files must be specially emphasized, because the calculation of retirement old-age insurance fund requires information on workers' employment and wage history. Administration efficiency should be raised and every means should be tried to reduce administrative expenses.

More regulations should be made for the second and third levels in regard to reporting financial statement and reserve fund investment situation regularly. A supervising body with auditing right should be set up to oversee whether contributions are timely put into the right accounts and whether old-age insurance is timely paid. When transferring the accumulated old-age insurance fund into annals, certain technical standards should be adopted so as to guarantee unified and just treatment for retirees.

A point worth special mentioning is that accurate and minute supervision should be made regularly to the entire old-age insurance system. The initial detailed forecast can only be based on long-term projections and necessary adjustment must be made after checking the initial forecast with accumulated experience. This requires the existence of a standardized statistic system, and the interval for detailed studies should not be more than three years.

(F) About old-age insurance in rural areas

Traditionally, the care of the old people in rural China rests on families, particularly sons. The implementation of family planning policies and the change in population development patterns make it necessary to strengthen social security support to old people in rural areas in the time ahead.

Experimentation in old-age insurance in rural areas began in 1986 and quickly expanded in scale soon after. Now two million people in 890 counties are taking part in the experiment. In one hundred of these counties, 80 percent of the farmers are now under insurance plans. The purpose of a rural old-age insurance system is to provide basic necessities in everyday life for old-age farmers who have lost the ability to work. It was then expected to popularize the insurance plan in 1995.

Those taking part in the plan pay 2 to 20 yuan (there are ten scales) a month to the insurance fund. Rural people in all trades take part in a unified insurance scheme. They can make the insurance payment every month or every year or at one lump sum at the beginning. Normally, the amount paid is 6 to 8 yuan per month. People with an annual income of 700 to 800 yuan for each member in the family are qualified to take part in the plan. The amount of pension is decided by the amount insured, the number of years insured and the return rate of the insurance fund. Farmers above 60 years usually receive an annual pension of 800 yuan. Farmers are to pay 80 percent of the insurance expense, while the other 20 percent is to be covered by collective funds or profits of rural enterprises. The income for insurance fund now is about one billion, and expected to grow to ten billion by 1995.

Both men and women start to receive subsidies released in the form of pensions at the age of 60. If the recipient dies before the age of 70, the rest of the pensions for the ten-year guaranteed period are issued to his or her surviving family members. Those who die after 70 continue to receive the pension. Old-age insurance in rural areas is in the charge of the county-level management body, which is responsible for taking care of the individual account of every insurer. The management fee is about 3 percent of the insurance fund.

The old-age insurance system in rural areas is the most basic form of protection for rural elders and the subsidy provided is very low. The varied practices in the system throughout the country are yet to be unified.

The flexibility of the regulations are designed to better suit the varied needs in different regions. Now it is necessary to unify and standardize the regulations and procedures for the rural old-age insurance system.

Apparently, the understanding of the nature, role and purpose of social security schemes in rural China is not very clear. Measures should be taken to extensively publicize information to help the rural population understand that there are many channels they can choose for taking part in the social security arrangement.

Though, the social security system is a rather recent development in rural China, speedy development has already been registered. This system has two advantages: one is subsidies from the collectives in addition to payment made by farmers themselves, and the other is that subsidies are issued in the form of old-age pensions. Whether the rural old-age insurance system will have a great impact on changing the poor conditions for old people in the countryside can only be determined in the future.

In short, the old-age insurance plan under study will further promote China's economic reform process. The basic purpose of the plan is to provide a basic level substitute for income for retired workers in urban areas, provided enterprises and workers are willing to make additional contributions. The plan has taken full consideration of the quick aging process of the Chinese population, and plans to establish an old-age insurance system that covers both urban and rural workers.

(2) The old-age insurance system should combine fairness with efficiency and take both into consideration.

The combination of fairness and efficiency should have more than one standard in various aspects of social security schemes.

During the reform, the degree and demand of fairness and efficiency reflected in various aspects of social security schemes are not the same. It will not be proper if we demand a single unified standard for every part of the schemes, be it social insurance, social relief or social welfare. Hainan Province had different standards in its reform of the social security system. As the nuclear part of social security, the social security system should better reflect the social insurance mechanism and give more emphasis to reciprocity and unification of the rights and obligations. The social security system is different from the demand for social relief and social welfare. The past social insurance system mixed up social welfare with social insurance. The kind of welfare security arrangement we have had always wants to have more security in the form of making available more offerings, and the result has been low efficiency. Here we should specially mention the past public funding for social insurance. That past system, admittedly, played a great role in balancing enterprise burdens and solving existing problems. It, however, had a serious drawback, i.e., rights and obligations were inconsistent. The issuing of old-age pensions was not linked with contributions toward the old-age pension fund. The consequence was not drawing resources from the rich to help the poor, but quite contrary, drawing resources from the poor to help the rich. Since the aging of the population is proportionate to the economic development level of a given region, the more developed is the economy, the more serious is the problem of aging of the population. Aging is most serious in economically developed areas such as Beijing, Shanghai and Jiangsu and least severe in such areas as Ningxia, Tibet and Yunnan. If old-age insurance is conducted as a national scheme, money from all over the country will be spent more in economically developed areas, resulting in the poor areas helping the developed areas. This is precisely a result of separating the rights and obligations of the system. Therefore, to have a uniform way of old-age insurance nationally does not bring fairness and efficiency. What it does is to make insurance fund payers and enterprises less enthusiastic, and twist the role of the three bodies of social security schemes. Such a system obviously cannot continue and should even less be blindly extended to a higher and wider scope.

It is entirely possible to organically combine fairness and efficiency with both aspects taken care of. For instance, the method of combining the issue of pensions with paying for the insurance brings together the rights and obligations, and is both equal and efficient. So long as fairness and efficiency are not forced together, but organically combined, both mechanisms, fairness and efficiency, can play their role at the same time.

The standards to be considered in combining fairness and efficiency in old-age insurance

Foreign experts put forward their opinions and questions in regard to the principles of fairness and efficiency during the discussions. Here are some standards which must be considered.

In terms of pensions, some minimum support should be provided to retirees or the disabled. This is to say that retirees and the disabled should not be left to live in poverty in order to guarantee basic social equality and justice.

Old-age pensions should be able to replace the former income which means that their living standard in retirement will not fall too much. This is an important standard we must keep in mind in designing old-age pension plans. Of course, pensions cannot substitute the entire income during the retirees' active working years. As a result, the plans designed should allow some difference in old-age pensions for those who have had higher income and those with lower incomes. The pension must be able to substitute part of the wage income. If the worker has a higher income, his old-age pension should also be higher.

The equality standards of different pension plans vary from region to region. The essential question here is how to combine the pension one enjoys with the money he has paid during his working years. The individual deposit plan is designed to enable workers to at least enjoy minumum life support after retiring. We may combine several methods to gether into one standard which should be both equal and acceptable to everybody.

Experiences of many countries have proved that workers do not necessarily receive pensions equal to the amount of their contributions. This is to say that what they pay and what they receive may not be the same. Now that China is implementing the method of individuals making the payment and workers should be made clear of the concept: they have to pay themselves.

A question related to equality is efficiency. Just like the question of equality, efficiency is also judged according to many standards.

One is that after the old-age pension system is in place, workers will work harder. Old-age pensions surely will have some effects on workers' enthusiasm, but it is not the only element. During discussions, it was felt that with old-age pensions, workers will work harder. The establishment of individual accounts will also cncourage workers to work harder. If the insurance fee toward old-age pensions and the income are combined, high income will bring higher pensions. There is some link between income and pensions, though such a link is not very clear.

There are several questions to consider. For a worker, he may not work till retirement age. How should we deal with such a question? What should we do if a worker is disabled or dies before his retirement? In many countries, the disabled and deceased pensions for the disabled worker or relatives of the deceased are associated with retirement pensions. In this regard, we should learn from their practices.

If inflation occurs, the old-age fund will devaluate. The drawing of old-age insurance plan should take into consideration the inflation index figure.

(3) Old-age security reform should take into consideration China's situation and practical status. A unified national scheme should be decided.

Reform plan for old-age social security system should take into consideration the dual economic structure and pluralistic social security schemes.

Reform of the old-age social security must be clear regarding two aspects: the dual economic structure and pluralistic social security schemes. The precondition for our studies is that the old-age pension in urban and rural areas we want to develop is based on different economic basis and different levels.

(A) The establishment of an old-age pension fund and the entire social security reform must take into consideration the following decisive factors:

It should be adaptable to the rapid aging process, at a high level, and with a quickening escalating nature. Aging in China is not as severe as forecast by the World Bank, the United Nations, the US Population Consulting Agency and some domestic institutions. We should proceed from scientific analysis and not get panic at the mentioning of the problem.

We should take into consideration provision for the old in urban and rural areas.

The goal of China's economic reform is to establish a socialist market economic system and old-age pension fund should be market-oriented.

We should combine world experiences with realities in China.

(B) Reform of the old-age pension system in urban areas

What do old people in urban areas live on:

	retirement pension	provided for by children	wages	total
cities	56%	22%	7%	85%
towns	48%	28%	7%	83%

Source of material: Sample Investigations Among Old People Above 60 in 1987, China.

The trend of change: the percentage of old people provided for by their children is dropping, and that of old people living on their own wages is going up. As old-age pensions increase in percentage, the state finance finds it difficult to continue this way.

The reform plan: to establish a retirement pension fund with money raised from the state, enterprises and individuals. It is very difficult for the state to produce a sum of seed money on top of already existing difficulties in paying increasing pensions. It is thus suggested that market economic measures be adopted and a social security share-holding bank be established.

The nature of the bank: both social security (mainly old-age pensions) and banking at the same time. To accumulate capital by selling shares and operate it as a bank, mainly for old-age insurance.

The operation principle of the bank: preparing fund by strictly following the share-holding system.

Loans and credit businesses like other banks should be conducted so as to quicken the increase in value of the capital. Individual payments for preparing receiving of old-age pension is to be put under individual accounts. There are two parts in the accounts: fixed sums (50 percent for example) from the time of opening of the account (for example when 25 years old) till retirement; another part is free to withdraw or make a deposit just like banks. The fixed sum of the old-age pension under the individual account will go up along with price index and increase in value at an interest rate 3 percent higher than long-term bank deposit. The social security share-holding bank operates under the supervision of the People's Bank of China and other departments concerned. All investment in production, social and welfare undertakings must bring profits. The system of risk responsibility should be implemented.

Plan for setting it up: From 1993 to 1995 is the preparation and experimental period during which the overall plan and implementation methods are drawn up. At the same time, where conditions are good, experiments should be conducted to gain experience for future popularization. Individual contributions to old-age preparation fund can begin when the contributor is 25 years old. Contributions can be made universally by deducting them from wages according to a certain percent. Before 35, the percentage can be 5 percent, and goes up to 8 percent after 35. In 1996, the practice should be popularized in the country. Those above 50 who are entitled to retirement pensions according to presently existing regulations, shall be exempted from the preparation fund. Those between 35 and 49 shall pay 3 percent of their wages and those between 25 and 34, 5 percent. Urban old-age pension regulations shall be made and effectively executed.

(C) Reform of the rural old-age pension system

What do old people in rural areas live on:

Provided for by rural undertakings:	68%
Depending on one's own labor earnings:	26%
Living on pensions:	1%
Total:	95%

(The source of these figures are the same as those about urban old people in the previous section.)

Direction of reform: Old-age care in rural areas should gradually move away from care by children to care by the society as in urban a as. One way to realize this is to establish social security share-holding banks, on self willingness; another way is to continue to advocate that young people should provide for their elderly, to hold back the speed of dismissing the role of families for taking care of the old as a result of commercial economy and rise of nuclear families; the third way is to promote comprehensive development of the population and community, develop an old-people care system that combines the collective and individual family efforts and strengthens community services; the fourth way is to develop insurance for single children and their parents, for instance, single children insurance fees can be turned into old-age insurance fund.

Social security system should respect the creativeness of the people.

Organized by the trade unions, workers in Shanghai set up two kinds of old-age additional insurance. One is to develop economic undertakings by the Retiree Management Committee. Now the economic undertakings by the Shanghai Retiree Management Committee are worth 1.5 billion yuan. Out of this, 1.4 billion yuan is made available as an additional insurance fund, resulting in paying additional benefits to a million retired workers. If such economic undertakings are developed throughout the country, they will make major contributions to China's social security system. Another is to subsidize old-age insurance. Still in Shanghai, apart from receiving benefits according to state regulations, every worker, at the time of retiring, receives one lump sum of subsidized old-age insurance fund of 10,000 yuan, or 20,000 yuan or even more. Old-age insurance should include several levels. In many countries, the basic old-age insurance benefits are very low, but we cannot lower the present level in China. While the basic insurance level cannot be lowered, we should have some caution in doing additional old-age insurance. Otherwise, if the insurance benefit level is pushed too high, or leads to compete in this area among the enterprises, the result will be disastrous.

In principle, China should have a nationally unified the old-age insurance system.

Whether there should be a nationally unified old-age insurance system? This question arouses different opinions.

Some experts believe the conditions for a nationally unified system are not ripe.

As a large country, China's economic development is not balanced among all regions. In Shanghai for example, the aging problem is very serious. It is natural that Shanghai wants a nationally unified system, since Shanghai turned in the past more profits to the state and now it should receive more for its old people from the central authorities. This, however, is not realistic. As a result, Shanghai has to take care of its own old people. Generally, wage levels in Shanghai are higher. And as a forerunner of reform, Shanghai has changed many formerly covered subsidies into part of the wages. Thus the percentages taken out of the total wages as old-age insurance fund can be rather low in Shanghai.

Most people support a nationally unified old-age insurance system.

Some specialists hold the position that it is not appropriate to only have national guidelines without national laws on social security schemes. Social security itself is a question of methods. Already there are different ways of fund raising and national legislation should take consideration of this fact. Now there are signs that management institutions are no longer the same in the country. The management of social security has been separated from labor departments, and is now under other departments or even the people's insurance companies. One recent proposal calls for trying out five or six foreign models in China.

Some specialists suggest the plans for raising old-age insurance fund and paying benefits, if not nationally unified, should have some uniformity within each locality. Some simply say the power of making those plans should rest with local governments. This involves the following questions: One, it is a question of whether the old-age insurance fund can well perform its role, if every locality is to have its own way of doing it and there is no coordination and mutual help among other regions; Two, how will the labor force move about if each locality is to have its own standards for raising and paying the fund. Specifically, some localities have individual accounts and some not. Some regions follow the complete accumulation model and others not. This is to say once we have entered the market economy, these questions are difficult to solve.

Still there are specialists who agree that the Ministry of Labor, while tackling the issue of social security, should also produce unified methods and unified management plans, which is in the interest of guaranteeing social justice. They also point out, however, the economic development is uneven and there is a great gap between the north and south. Under such circumstances, how to find a good solution needs further study.

2. The Old-Age Insurance System and the Raising and Spending of the Old-Age Insurance Fund

(1) It is necessary to establish a multi-level old-age insurance system. Questions to consider are how to broaden the coverage, raise the old-age care standard and make the transition from the old to the new system.

A major content in China's reform of the traditional old-age care system is to change the single form of old-age pension scheme to a multi-level old-age insurance plan.

The multi-level old-age care scheme proposed by the Ministry of Labor is a good model.

Some international commentators have pointed out that there are rather complete three-level or multi-level insurance systems in industrialized nations. For example, Japan, Switzerland, Britain and the United States have adopted such multi-level insurance systems. The basic level is created for stability, the second is for vocational welfare care. And individuals may choose any one of them. In developing countries, there is usually only one level of social security scheme or even if there is a second level, it exists only in name. Trends of development, however, point to more standardization of the second level. We should consider the establishment of both levels since after all they compliment each other.

The present system in China is a mono-level one. The plan of the Ministry of Labor is to replace the old with a new system, which is to consist of three levels. The first or basic level should include two parts, one is to be built on the basis of the average wages in the entire city or province and the second part is to link up with the amount of money and length of service one makes during the lifetime. The second level is purely a system of accumulation which is to be established where the accounts are opened by enterprises according to their performance. The third level is purely established by individuals, which is going to be a special form of account transfer. It is going to a system that sets a standard for welfare fund and the amount to be turned in.

Every plan has its strong and weak points, but on the whole they constitute a good model.

Specifically, funds contributed at the first level are exempt from tax, which is not true for the second level. It is a common practice to increase the effectiveness of such plans through the method of tax exemption for the employer. This system of course is to transfer the standard wages based on basic care to total wages which is required by wage reforms. The proposal of the Ministry of Labor is not detailed enough as it does not explicitly explain the exact welfare level and substituting rate. On this point, we can take a look at some of the state regulations. The No. 102 Document discusses social security's minimum level and the No. 128 Document deals with old-age pension and welfare care for the disabled and survivors of the deceased. Both documents demand that the minimum level of welfare care be at 40 percent and 45 percent of the wage.

Welfare plans in some developed nations vary from region to region in their countries.

China's Central Government once issued a document numbered 33, which proposed a multi-level welfare system, with the purpose of establishing some kind of basic welfare care. It means that there should be a guarantee of minimum welfare care, or welfare care linked up with making money. The idea is to link up both levels, one is what is provided by the employer and the other is savings on individual's initiative. Both are basically individual accounts. Practices in China vary from place to place. For example, none of the plans existing in Hainan, Shenzhen and Xiamen are in conformity with state guidance plans.

Take Shenzhen for example. Shenzhen has proposed a plan to fundamentally switch to individual accounts. Some people stand for having individual accounts, arguing that such accounts include all the basic fund, giving basic guarantees for dealing with problems of old age in future. However, most places in China have problems with establishing individual accounts. Even if they believe that it is a good idea to have individual accounts, they are not willing to do so. Some places have adopted the pay-as-you-go system. The cost for executing the present welfare care system is very high. If a region wants to replace the old system with a kind of new individual accounts, it has to have an appropriate amount of capital to pay back all the old-age insurance fund. Besides, it has to put up funds for establishing individual accounts. In other words, the up front capital will greatly increase in order to facilitate the transition from the present system to a new individual account system. Shenzhen may be the only place in China to practice this kind of transition, since the city has fewer retired workers, carries less burden under the existing system, and has a fairly large amount of accumulated capital.

Four years ago, Hainan Province made a very similar proposal as the one from Shenzhen. The main idea was that Hainan should also transit from the present system to an individual account system. Plans coming more recently from Hainan do not call for complete transition to individual accounts. The individual account system is only one of several levels in a new system. Besides, there is the welfare fund system, which is closely linked with making money and a welfare system which is related to the record of making money during the entire lifetime. The basic level must at least be a pay-as-you-go arrangement. As a result, total costs may be high when establishing the individual account system, it will not, however, be more costly than a system of entirely relying on a fund.

The design of a multi-level old-age care system should have a broad coverage and raise the standard of such care.

It is important to have a multi-level old-age care system which involves two aspects: one is how such care should broaden its coverage and the other is how to effectively improve the standard of such care. And both issues involve the question of having multi-level care for the following reasons: (a) Old people also have their different age groups and their population will increase progressively till the year of 2040; Urban and rural places are on different levels, just as the southeast, northwest and central China all differ from each other and are spread out in a shape like a ladder. (b) Economic development levels are not the same from region to region and there are differences even within each region. The southeast and coastal areas have experienced a much faster development than the northwest. (c) The process of reform has also been carried out at different levels. Consequently, the reform of old-age care should also be conducted at different levels.

Then how to divide the levels? It should be realized that it is workable to have the retirement pension fund in urban areas drawn together. In urban areas, retirement pensions now make up 56 percent of the economic resources for the old people, which is a large percentage. Whether the raising of this fund should be done nationally or at different levels is a question worth studying. Rural reform has to be carried out on the status quo. For old people in rural areas, 67 percent of their economic resources are provided by their children, while their labor income only makes up 26 percent. The rest comes from government subsidies, help from relatives and friends, provisions from their spouses and in a very small minority of villages retirement pensions, as some rural enterprises and some scattered villages practice a retirement system. These ratios cannot change no matter what reforms there are. In the point of view of development, Chinese families are becoming smaller and the provisions from children will gradually drop in percentage. It is, therefore, necessary to find ways to introduce the retirement system in rural areas in order to take care of the old people. We have made different experiments, but under conditions of a market economy, there will not be an appropriate method unless we take the approach of combining insurance with banks. This calls for having life insurance banks.

Apart from the problem of inflation, which must be solved, ways must be found to increase the income of old people, in order to improve the level of old-age care. For instance, old people should be employed for appropriate jobs in order to increase their income. There is a lot that can be done in China in this aspect.

A new insurance system should be created for young workers while subsidies should be paid by the state for the welfare fund of already retired workers.

In the long run, a new insurance system should be created for young workers. On the other hand, state-owned enterprises or the government should offer subsidies to the welfare fund for already retired workers. For workers still active on jobs, a bonus method should be implemented to encourage them to willingly take part in the new system.

To some extent, the picture of a new mechanism of social security for the old people is getting clear in China. It is now a common understanding that China's move toward a market economy is in the interest of a multi-level social security system. At the basic level, income from social security schemes should remain low while additional income can come from the second level. This is a model based on the stabilization of the society and a pay-as-you-go mechanism. The second level is the individual accounts or a system of raising all the money needed. In view of China's development, the second level should occupy the major part of the social security arrangement. At present, insurance fees are contributed by the employee and the employer after tax exemptions by the government according to law.

From a long-term point of view, it is not hard to imagine another level. This is to say to clearly define an insurance fund, establish a long-term target and come up with the rate of insurance fees required by realizing the target. On the basis of long-term planning, Singapore carefully did this by defining insurance fees and health care expenses. The latter guarantees that individuals and their family members are taken care of once they get old and live in retirement. What are the insurance fees for people with different incomes? Singapore divided monthly income into five groups and made plans for each group: how much health insurance money was going to be needed by the man and his wife when they are old? How much money would he need to buy a house on installment and with a mortgage? How much money should he save so that he would have enough to support a period of twenty years living in retirement. Calculations from the then existing interest rate and wage increase rate finally suggested that the long-term insurance fee rate should be 40 percent. Only with such a figure, would there be 4 percent health insurance, 24 percent of housing insurance and 10 percent of retirement insurance. In China, we can also make similar planning with similar estimated index figures, though the certainty of the figures may be slightly smaller. When making long-term target planning, it is best to come up with the figure of the insurance fee rate required, and then implement the system with a fixed framework. At the beginning, the rate of insurance fees may be slightly low and the distribution of the insurance fund should be strictly controlled. Later along with the quickening of economic growth, the rate can be raised gradually. It is not going to be difficult to do so when the economy is in the growth period. Besides, relatively higher rates of insurance fees can play the role of stabilizing the micro-economy, because when wages are high, it is natural to spend part of the money on old-age retirement insurance. This will help reduce consumption and control inflation.

Things now are different in China. According to recent research results, China has a huge retired population of 24 million. Taking care of them is an obligation for the nation and the responsibility to pay old-age insurance to the retired is a task left by history. To examine carefully, one will see that the retirement insurance fund that has to be paid does exist, except it is scattered and mixed under different listings. China is in need of money, and there are two solutions based on theoretical analysis and practical foundations.

First, people must ask the question of where the old-age insurance fund for the retired has gone to. In principle, state-owned enterprises could have set aside funds for them in the past thirty years for their use in retirement. However, the question is profits of the state-owned enterprises have been mixed up together with state budgets and there is no independent account to say specifically who owns what. Where have the profits gone to then? They have become fixed assets of state-owned enterprises, or they have been invested, through state budgets, into the construction of the infrastructure such as harbors, airports and roads. Or they have been spent on housing and other construction projects. If this is indeed the situation, the money can be found and recovered. And then this fund which is not hidden in different forms among various assets of the Central Government can be spent on paying retirement pensions. One possibility is to link it up with enterprises reform, such as the capital from selling some assets as shares can be used to pay pensions. Another possibility is to collect infrastructure fees such as road tolls and spend it on pensions. The third possibility is to link it up with housing reform. The publicly built houses all belong to the state. House rent now is very low. Since rent is not fixed according to a market, renting houses cannot become a market operation, making the return on house building very low. Experiments may be made by establishing house renting markets and income from house rent can be used to cover the debts of retirement pensions.

Second, there should be just rationales, both theoretical and practical, for present young workers to pay old-age insurance funds for already retired workers. The rationale we have now is what Singapore once has put forward, i.e., to make up what old people deserve to have. Young workers now start working under favorable conditions, as they enjoy a relatively developed infrastructure, capital accumulation and fixed assets, so that they can have relatively high production capability and on that basis have higher income. All the infrastructure and capital accumulation come from contributions by the old generation of workers, who did not receive the benefits generated by the productivity based on accumulated capital. In this sense, it is natural that a certain amount of income is drawn from the wages of young workers to contribute to the old-age insurance fund for the retired workers.

There is the question of how workers still working now naturally and normally can be transferred into the new system. To give bonus to these workers may be one way to encourage them to willingly transfer into the new system. Specifically there are three methods.

One, suppose a worker has been working under the old system for X number of years, and in this case, say ten years. Then the total old-age insurance money can be calculated and frozen. Then he goes into the new system and continues to pay insurance. By the time of his retirement, the frozen amount is paid back to him. Now he can immediately be part of the new system and the insurance fee in that ten years can be changed into cash and invested. All benefits from it is his.

Two, a calculation should be made to know his X number of years should have Y sum of stipend, which is put into his individual account. Then he can begin paying insurance under the new system and start to accumulate money.

Three, a long-term insurance fee rate can be estimated from the Y sum of money he has paid. This rate may be very low. Then he can continue to follow a relatively low insurance fee rate. He can make payment of insurance fee at the low rate together with the present old-age insurance payment. After some years, there will not be much difference between what he is going to receive from that of others.

Old-age care fund for the retired and still active workers can be drawn by issuing bonds and land use rights.

Some specialists abroad are doubtful if some way can be found to deal with the rights of stocks in the enterprises (rights brought about by old-age care) held by the retired and presently still working workers. To deal with this issue, there is the hypothesis to have stocks issued to the retired and still active workers in the enterprises. That is to say, as far as the old-age care fund is concerned, one way is to guarantee that enterprises benefit from its profits, rather than to try to sell its assets, during the transition to the market economic mechanism. In reality, it means to support the investment we are talking about with ownership rights. This hypothesis may well suit the Chinese concept of collective involvement.

There are also specialists who suggest land use rights may be sold to generate money for old-age care funds for retired and still active workers. This involves a preparation fund which can be considered from two angles. One is the responsibility we have for those workers who worked under the system of the planned economy till their retirement. The other is how to deal with the question of an aging population. Among the suggestions concerning a preparation fund is to find the fund accumulated together by workers who worked under the old mechanism, including fixed assets, enterprises and infrastructure. One point can be added, i.e., to sell the right to use land in large Chinese cities can generate cash more easily and quickly.

(2) The choice of fund raising models and payment levels should be based on conditions in China and be reasonable.

A number of ways should be adopted to draw old-age insurance fund.

Internationally, there are three models for raising money for old-age insurance fund: complete accumulation, another is partial accumulation and pay-as-you-go. There have been varied opinions during discussions as to which model China should take. But the general consensus is to adopt the partial accumulation method, which better suits China's conditions.

Why should China adopt the partial accumulation method?

Of the three ways, pay-as-you-go obviously will not work in China, and almost no one in China agrees with it. The complete accumulation, or complete fund model, can stand aging of the population. Its reliance on economic means is conducive to mobilizing the enthusiasm of those who pay the fees. Another advantage is that this method can raise a great sum of funds. Simply put, this method will provide money for use which is most attractive to departments in charge of taking care of the old. It does, however, have three main drawbacks: one, there is no coordination among participants in the system, which is not in conformity with the principle of mutual help in social security schemes, and will surely result in great gaps between high and low. Two, it will lead to the paying of past debts by the already retired, the retiring and those still working. A simple estimate shows if the debts paid by the three groups are put together, they will amount to be 42 percent of total wages. This means all the enterprises will have to pay money at the 42 percent rate and do so for several years (in order to divide past debts to a paying period of several years). The paying process will stretch for twenty years, which is too much of a burden for enterprises. Three, the fund is difficult to spend. How large will the fund be? Estimates have been done, but no accurate figures have been derived. If the complete fund method is adopted, by the year 2020, the total accumulated fund will be 20,000 billion yuan. The GNP then will be 17,000 billion yuan. Many people say there can never be a fund as large as 20,000 billion yuan. At best, it is a bluff by the calculator. Such a suggestion is wrong. In Singapore, the fund exceeded its GNP in a very short period. The question is as Singapore is a small country with a population of 2.9 million, its fund is easy to spend. For China with a population of 1.1 billion, the funds will be too huge to properly spend.

Repeated discussions and comparisons of the three models finally led people to approve the partial accumulation method. When the United States established its social security system in the 1930s, it was on the whole prepared to adopt the complete fund method. Inflation and operation of the fund and other factors prevented the establishment of the system until 1939 and 1940 when actually the partial accumulation model was adopted. In Germany and Japan, there has been a similar process. Before World War II, France also adopted the partial accumulation method. After the war, a national discussion on the funding model took place. Upon analysis, people believed that France could take the pay-as-you-go method given the funding conditions and historical factors. Britain, or British Commonwealth countries in particular, mostly took the partial accumulation method. China may not take any of the two extreme methods, but instead take the middle approach.

China's adoption of the partial accumulation method is based on its own conditions.

Some international specialists, having studied methods in foreign countries, and analyzed fund raising methods in China, suggested that China adopt the partial accumulation method. A look at Europe at the end of last century and early this century shows that in Germany, social security was introduced for employees and individuals and employers enjoyed insurance fund according to the principle for individual distribution. This was the fundamental principle for the social security system. Initially, a method of complete funding took shape. As more and more people became part of the system, problems began to surface for the "complete fund raising" concept. Later during World War II, inflation and other factors totally exhausted the fund reserves of the social security plan. In fact, the system was approaching maturity. Switching to the pay-as-you-go method on that basis was then natural. As a result, the pay-as-you-go method practice by industrialized nations, with a few exceptions, has been efficient. This could be described as the first plan.

The second plan was the "employer initiated plan" or "individual security plan." It could be based on a general or complete fund raising method. There have been exceptions, too. France's second plan based on the pay-as-you-go method was very unusual. The first plans in industrialized nations were, therefore, based on the pay-as-you-go model.

In developing nations, we may find that some of them, mostly in Latin America, introduced social security schemes before World War II. They copied the entire Europe model of public funds and then fell back to a partial-fund system because of inflation and the equalitarianism in the distribution of insurance fund (as equalitarianism was not in conformity with the increase in distribution demand).

Other developing countries, mostly in Asia, Africa and the Caribbean, developed social security plans after World War II. They followed two methods: those countries which adopted a limited insurance fund plans generally follow the partial-fund system, while the rest which are prepared to adopt the fund system followed the complete fund system. Here, being "prepared to adopt the fund system" in definition means completely raising public funds. Generally speaking, we can say that the models for developing nations include general, complete and partial raising of public funds, while developed nations all based their plans on the pay-as-you-go method.

With this background in mind, we should now take a look at the situation in China. First, China is a developing country, but China did not start from nothing, as in the case of some developing countries which had no past obligations and had no elderly that had ever received pensions. China started from a plan based on pay-as-you-go model, which has been in practice for nearly forty years. As a result, China has rights and insurance funds that should have been paid. Those who are to receive old-age pension are there, but there is no corresponding old-age fund. On average, the pay-as-you-go insurance fund, at about 12 to 13 percent, is at its lowest level, which is different from other developing countries.

Other major factors include the fast aging of the Chinese population, which is very unusual for a developing country. Bearing all this in mind, we have come to the conclusion that the method cannot be one of complete fund. For the first-level plans, there are several possibilities, but in reality, some must be excluded. One is the pay-as-you-go method. It is entirely possible to continue with this method, but it will mean the distribution rate has to be raised with each passing year, making it inconvenient in terms of management. Besides, under such a system, the final distribution rate can be very high, especially with the emergence of an aging population.

As for other fund raising methods, if we do not adopt the complete fund method, it means we will have to immediately increase or make investment of a capital equivalent to insurance funds receivable, which cannot be done in practice.

The third method is to raise money through a certain level of insurance fund. This means there are stable insurance fund resources and a precondition, i.e., under such system, material capital reserve will accumulate. The question is if a high distribution rate can be tolerated? Another question is that is there, or will there be, a great and suitable investment market that draws huge amounts of accumulated capital? In theory, all the above plans are possible, but they all create various kinds of problems. So now we should turn to consider the partial fund raising system, which has been practiced in many developing countries.

The partial fund system means you do not have to accumulate enough capital in order to pay all the due debts, but rather you can use the accumulated fund to pay only part of the debts. Even though, there are still many requests. A condition that the Ministry of Labor examined and used is to establish a system under which you can continue to add a debt to the pay-as-you-go insurance fund. Of course there are other methods, too.

Another fund raising method that has been applied by many countries is called the "staircase insurance fund system." It maintains the continuity of time intervals on the distribution curve. Within these time intervals, the level of insurance fund will determine a certain standard, generally the capital reserve standard. For instance, it may be a standard like the following: we need a non-decrease capital reserve so that we can make long-term investment and, therefore, we do not have to draw principal from it.

Another fund raising method is to fix the capital reserve level at certain times of the insurance fund distribution expenses. It can be twice or three times or any other times as much.

Where should the accumulated fund based on the partial accumulation model be kept? What should be the standards for accumulation?

Now that people have reached a common ground on making the partial accumulation as the fund rasing model, there are two concrete questions to consider. One is where should the partial accumulation fund be kept, in the "big pot," or "small pot" or both? Which should be the main form? This question came up in the plans of all provinces. If the entire fund is deposited in a social public accumulation account, how effective will it work? If a part of the fund is placed in a "small pot," what will be the result? It is a question worth studying.

The second question is whether the accumulation fund should be large or small? Shall it be very large, or small or somewhere in the middle? At what level should it be controlled? People may tend to agree that at the beginning of the reform, the accumulation fund should be kept at a low level. The level should be appropriate to the degree of development of our capital market. This is correct in theory, but exactly how it should be maintained in practice is still a question. Some foreign specialists proposed that a 3-percent (out of the total wages) public accumulation fund is the ideal level. Then there is the question of on what standards and reasons is this percentage based? At this stage, we still do not have an exact figure of how much fund there will be to be made use of in the capital market. In Hainan Province, the social public fund will be between one and two billion yuan by the year 2000, according to the high level of the three-level—high, medium and low—formula. This figure only refers to the amount kept in the big social public accumulation account, and is derived by initial calculation in the absence of complete data. So the question we face is still shortage of capital rather than having no place to spend the fund.

The standard for partial accumulation should be fully based on the capability of China'e economy, or approximately about 3 percent of the total wages.

In deciding the models for raising fund, we should fully take into consideration the capability of the Chinese economy. First, China now persists in having public ownership as the main sector of the economy. The economic efficiency of state-owned sector is still at a low ebb and the burden is still too heavy. It is thus necessary to make a rational choice between the target of economic growth and the target for fund raising for social security. If too much money is raised for social security, apparently the economy at present cannot bear it. Second, it will still be some time before the capital market can mature in China. Investment returns are now low, and the state banks are already hard pressed to pay interest to deposits made by the public. Under such a situation, if the scale of fund raising for social security schemes is too large, it will lead to a result contrary to the design. That is to say the choice of the fund raising model and the scale of its accumulation should develop simultaneously with the maturity of the Chinese capital market. Third, in the decade before the end of the century, China will be in a quick development period, during which the pressure of inflation will be serious, posing great problems to the maintenance of the value of the accumulated fund. In conclusion, we should have a very careful attitude toward the accumulation of a social security fund. At present, the aging problem for the Chinese population is not the severest in the world, but the funds raised for old-age pensions is nearly 20 percent of the average national total wages. By mid-21st century, the aging problem will be more obvious. For China the question is what percentage out of the total wages should be drawn into the pension fund.

Once partial accumulation is decided to be the model, the selection of the accumulation rate becomes a crucial question.

Firstly, we have to decide whether to take the smooth or the staircase method. In Japan, the rate goes up every five years. Initially, we thought China should also take the staircase method like Japan, though the period for the escalation may not be five years, as it can either be three years or more than five years, depending on the development of the economy. The advantage is that the impact and effect on enterprises will be small. Secondly, the accumulation rate must be accurately calculated and quantitative analyses made. Relatively speaking, this is a rather weak area in China. We rarely make careful analyses of hundreds of thousands and even millions of data. In the future, departments should act like doctors getting together to study the figures. The final decision should be based on the result of quantitative analysis. Concretely, the accumulation rate in China should be about 3 percent of total wages in the country. This projection is proposed after studies of the domestic situation and international practices, as well as the present level of revenue and expenditure. The accumulation fund from the workers hired by contracts is roughly 3 percent, in some cases, 2.9 percent and 3.1 percent of the total wages. If this figure is taken as the accumulation rate for the partial accumulation model, it will not add any burden to the financial departments and enterprises.

Forecast of partial accumulation degree demands careful work.

Though partial accumulation clearly does not suggest complete accumulation, it does however carry the meaning of being extensive. In fact, the pay-as-you-go model, when starting from zero, can also be viewed as an extreme form of partial accumulation. The term partial accumulation includes the whole process between zero and complete accumulation. Then where should it be placed in this process, in the middle or exactly where? This is a highly flexible question.

It should be explained that when making actual forecasts, the total wages and total pensions should first be estimated, since this is the starting point. Once these two figures are available, some projections should be made, including investigations of typical cases, sample demographic census, and the calculation of the number of new workers and the rate of wage increases. When all this information is at hand, one can start with making a series of plans, such as a plan for the tax rate of insurance funds to remain unchanged for a period of five years. After that, it may remain at the same level for seven years and further on, nine years.

Old-age pensions should neither be too high at the beginning nor lower than the existing level.

The level of old-age pensions is a very important question in the old-age insurance plan. And it is worth studying as to which level can be said to be in conformity with the situation in China. Many specialists hold the view that the level should not be set too high, since it is very difficult to lower once it is set. Instead, it is very easy to raise it. Besides, the lower the level, the more extensively it can be applied and more possible to be extended to the whole country. At present, however, it is impossible to set the level lower than the existing figure, at which level 140 million workers are receiving the pension. All projections should be based on this present figure.

To decide the level of old-age pensions, the following three questions (or three relationships) should be handled well.

The first is the relationship between the level of old-age pensions as well as the guarantee of basic living standard and the income level when workers are on the job. In other words, the level of old-age pensions should not be too low, whether from the point of view of the basic need of social security (or common law) or because social security acts as a stabilizer and a safety network of the society. It is just like the case of the market economy, which protects competition and the strong and thus has a stabilizing function.

The second is the relationship between the level of old-age pensions and the ability to endure it economically. China has a large population and a weak economic foundation. It should, therefore, "live frugally first and enjoy affluence later." In this sense, the standards for old-age pensions should not be high. We should particularly learn from the lessons of welfare states and not unrealistically set high levels for oisld-age pensions.

The third is the relationship between the level of old-age

pensions and the pension level that has been in existence. The system has been implemented for forty years under the planned economic system. It has a whole series of its own methods. Whether they are correct or wrong, they have been in existence for four decades. Then what's the present level? In 1991, the retirement pension in China was 1,936 yuan on average with that for workers retired from state-owned enterprises being 2,096 yuan. People still argue on the issue whether such figures are too high or too low. The theoretical circles in particular believe this is too high for the state to manage. Of course many others say it is too low. No matter what, its existence is an objective fact. Conceptually speaking, there is a hard rule that pension can only go up because of its inertia or the comparing phenomenon. The situation in China is that we must proceed from this reality and make analyses from the angle of whether it is doable.

3. The Operation and Management of the Old-Age Insurance Fund

(1) Investment operations of old-age insurance fund should guarantee safety and investment earning rate.

Criteria for investing old-age insurance fund: safety and earning rate

The basic decisive factors for investing the old-age insurance fund are safety and earning rate. The importance of rate of turnover is a second consideration, so long as the fund increases in value. The earnings should at least be more than the present inflation rate, otherwise, the fund will experience losses. When the reserve fund is generated from the partial accumulation method, which combines wages with old-age pensions, it is also of equal importance if the nominal earning rate is higher than the rate of wage increase.

There are other important factors, too, such as investment must be made in projects that are sound, both economically and socially. There are some basic ground rules for governing the investment of old-age insurance fund. The reality in China now is that the old-age fund has made certain sums of reserves, but the fund so far has been put in the bank or used to buy national bonds. These bonds, apparently, will not generate returns higher than the inflation rate, which means the fund is not increasing in value. This raises a question: in the process of reforming the social security system, should there be a fund system based on accumulated reserves. How should the reserve funds be invested? Can they be used for positive investment? Will the national economy be able to absorb the accumulated funds? Can they be made to support production? In reality, therefore, accumulations have direct bearings on the increasing burdens that come along with the aging of the population.

Now about the management of the old-age fund plans at the three levels. As for the first level, the finances must be self-governed. In other words, they should be separated from government budgets. There should be the freedom to invest the fund, so as to ensure the interests of the insurers to the maximum degree. As for the second and third levels, there should apparently be more necessary supervision, so as to ensure proper use of the funds. At the first level, there is a tacit government guarantee: interest will be paid back. There is, however, no such guarantee at the second and third levels. Proper and efficient management for investing old-age insurance fund at the second and third levels, therefore, are of great importance.

If the old-age insurance fund cannot receive actual earnings, those who have made their contributions to the funds will gradually lose the money. Thus management is very essential. And bookkeeping must be well done, recording the exact contributions insurers have made. Laws in regard of this must be made. The account books of these funds should be made public to facilitate public inquiries.

So long as investment is correctly made, the earning rate for investing old-age insurance fund will be very high.

Investment in China is closely associated with the entire process of the growth of Chinese economy and the development of the financial market and investment market. To study China's investment, one must first study the economic development stage and the situation in the monetary and financial markets. Experiences of Japan, Singapore and some others indicate that the accumulated capital from old-age insurance fund deposit is very important in the initial stage of economic development. In the past, in Japan and Singapore and now in China, there are the same issues: low income, low deposit rate and private ownership of capital. Large sums of capital are badly needed in construction of the infrastructure such as power stations, telecommunications, expressways, harbors, airports, public housing and industrial facilities. As a result, deposits are always short of demand. Unless some promotion measures are taken, the economy may fall into a low-level balance and will not experience high speed growth.

Like a car waiting for ignition, sometimes you have to offer some help. Once it is started, it will go forward by the factor of inertia. The incentive for accumulating capital is a high interest rate, which will lead to individual investment and direct foreign investment. If all the old-age fund is mobilized, plus government loans and national bonds issued by the Ministry of Finance, there is a solid foundation for the construction of infrastructure and future growth. The final result is a sound cycle of speedy economic growth, high taxation, high income tax and high company tax.

At the beginning, the use of old-age insurance fund was under the management of the central bank in Singapore. By mid-1980s, the sum had become so large that it led to an independent management organ called "governmental investment company," which specially manages various kinds of old-age insurance funds. Underneath the companies, there are investment banks led directly by the cabinet for making investment overseas, such as buying US government bonds, German's Marks, Japanese shares and Australian real estate. This is a process from accumulating huge sums of domestic funds to making overseas investments and accumulating foreign exchange.

To guarantee real earnings, it is imperative to keep the rate of nominal earnings higher than the inflation rate. If you have made a correct investment, and promoted the increase of your investment, you will surely receive satisfactory earnings. In Singapore, the government used to fix earning rates to guarantee real earnings. In the thirty years before the capital market was fully developed there, retired workers and all those taking part in the insurance schemes enjoyed a fixed earning rate at approximately 1.5-2 percent.

Once the capital market became mature, the control on the interest rate lessened and the exchange rate was allowed to fluctuate with the international capital market. Interest arbitrage on the international market can also keep the earnings higher than the rate of inflation. In fact, most of Singapore's retirement fund in the past ten years has been invested abroad. With such investment in huge sums, Singapore not only has learned technology and knowledge, but also earned annual interests of 15 to 20 percent. As the government only pays 6 to 7 percent interest on bonds, the net income from such investment is obvious. In fact, even the 6 to 7 percent of interest is still 2 to 3 percent higher than inflation. The earning rate of 15 to 20 percent from investment abroad brings the government an income of several billion US dollars. The case in Singapore proves that so long as it is correctly managed, there will be earnings from investment and the earnings can be very high.

Theoretically speaking, China is a country with a surplus labor force but a shortage of capital, which means the capital earning rate must be very high. The marginal productivity of the capital should be very high. How does this happen in practice? While capital pours into China from all parts of the world. For instance, Mr. X from Hong Kong invests in road building in China, some US company buys, with old-age insurance fund, the asset of the Hong Kong company which has invested in China, Singaporean investors invest their capital—even including income from selling houses—to China's Fuzhou, Hong Kong and Taiwan, trying to profit from manufacturing production, plants and real estate. This means the earning rate in China must be very high, otherwise, there will not be so many investors. However, why the earning rate is lower than inflation at present? The main reason lies in the chaos in the system. Once things are straightened out within the system, the actual productivity of the capital and real earning rate will be high.

The operation of old-age insurance fund should be decentralized and diversified.

Some specialists ask once the fund has accumulated to a certain sum, which will be the better way to operate, in a unified or diversified way? Which will generate higher earning? Which suits the condition in China better? Which is more appropriate to China's ability of making use of capital and the degree of maturity of China's capital market? The capital market in China is far from perfect in terms of its function. It has not reached maturity. Against this background, diversified operation should be the choice. The role of the Central Government should be making policies.

Investment of the old-age insurance fund should promote economic development and management of such investment should be strengthened.

We should learn from the lessons and experiences of Latin American countries in managing the investment of social security funds. Their experiences are particularly useful to us because we are all developing countries. Earnings from investment from social security schemes of partial or complete fund in most countries have not been satisfactory, for several reasons. First, there is the inflation problem. Second, some countries did not effectively prevent the abuse of social security funds. Such funds should not be used to make up government deficits or public expenditure. Third, some investment structures are not reasonable, which leads to problems in the direction of investment. All of these should be our lessons. Furthermore, the absence of a relatively sophisticated capital or monetary market in many Latin American countries is another reason for low earning rates. When we think of the question of increasing the value of investment, we should consider how to combine investment with promoting economic development and the establishment and maturity of the capital market, so as to bring about a sound circle. This is because the final solution of social security lies in economic development.

(2) Management of the old-age insurance fund

The principles of independence and supervision

There are two principles for the management of the old-age insurance fund: one is independence and the other supervision. How to increase the value of the fund should be a solution independent from government decisions. There have been many suggestions in China, but none has been put into practice, because problems have already occurred in certain areas. China now has accumulated a capital of 15 billion yuan, which can disappear from the bank in a matter of one or two months. The people's bank, or the central bank, seems to be less interested in this fund. The commercial and industrial bank, the investment bank and its trust investment bank wish to make use of the fund. The departments which can make the decision is less enthusiastic. As for the question of supervision, the total sum of 15 billion yuan (less the sum that has been used to buy national bonds, there are still 12 to 13 billion yuan) has so far been managed relatively well. Of course, there are always problems as there are more than two thousand counties in China. We do not have a very sound management system, nor effective supervision and auditing methods. People are studying how to control the fund. Some people suggest foundations be set up. Others say an authoritative and independent management organ should be established. All these suggestions are worth pondering for democratic management in the future.

Measures should be taken to address the question of inadequate supervision and examination of the management of the old-age insurance fund.

Supervision and examination of the management of old-age insurance fund in China are not adequate, and measures should be taken to correct the situation. Some of the measures Singapore has adopted include:

One, a strict system for employers to make the payment has been adopted. Employers have to make monthly payments into the insurance fund and the record is kept by computers. If they fail to make the payment within fourteen days, they can be brought to court or fined heavily. This system makes the life of those who dare to delay or evade payment miserable.

Two, a strict accounting examination system has been adopted. Every six months, management staff will receive balance sheets on amounts of payment, credit and loans and interest. Whether they are at home or abroad, they can use a secret telephone to check the accounts at anytime. As a result, whoever twists the figures will immediately be discovered.

Individual account also suits China's basic old-age insurance

There are now two problems with China's old-age insurance system: one is the small scale of coverage, since there is no old-age insurance for rural areas and the non-public sector, and the other is the over-expansive coverage in state-owned enterprises. To establish a national old-age insurance scheme, we cannot follow the practice in state-owned enterprises. What we should look for is a scheme that covers the whole society and facilitates the flow of the labor force at the same time. In this regard, the individual account system is a good choice. In Shanghai, for example, more and more people have gone there from rural areas to look for jobs. These rural workers do not have old-age insurance coverage. With individual accounts, their contribution made while working in Shanghai can be taken home when they leave Shanghai. The individual account system, therefore, not only is suitable to people working under different ownerships, but also in both urban and rural areas.

The management of the old-age insurance fund should be unified nationally, but it is very difficult to carry out.

Many people stand for the unified administration of the management system. In reality, however, this is very difficult to realize. Firstly, there are differences in opinion among departments and frictions often occur. Secondly, if industrial injury, old-age, unemployment insurance are all managed as separate insurance items, the result will be more payment imposed on enterprises, which in turn increases production costs and lowers economic efficiency. To be free from departmental clashes, and to avoid additional burdens on enterprises, old-age insurance should be done nationally. There are, however, two very difficult problems. One is that the central and local governments have their own interests to look after. The other is fund raising for old-age insurance in the past started from the grassroots level, unlike other countries, where fund raising is done according to national laws. As a result, in many localities, it is very difficult to have the county governor, the city mayor or any local government official agree to turn in the money to a higher or central organ. In spite of this, unification of management must be implemented. What is more difficult is the unification of contribution rate. Finally, there is the difficulty of finding enough qualified managerial staff and a sophisticated management system. We are still in a primary stage where problems exist in all aspects, including archive keeping, auditing, accounting and statistics. As for personnel, there are 28,000 people working in 2,900 organs. This percentage falls short of the international figure by dozens of times. In France for instance, there are 200,000 people working at management levels for a population which is only 5 percent of that in China. Of course the percentage of rural population in China is much higher than in France, still more people should be put to work in old-age insurance management institutions.

Chapter III
China's Unemployment Insurance System

1. The Present Situation, Problems and Principles for Reform

(1) China's labor force increases at an annual rate of 1.3 percent. Reform of the labor system, the rational flow of the labor force and social stability require the establishment of an unemployment insurance system.

The total labor force at the end of 1990 was 567 million, 75 percent of which lives in rural areas (See Table 1).

Table 1 China's Labor Force in 1990 (Unit: million)

Employed by the state	103.5
Employed by collectives in urban areas	35.5
Employed by others	1.6
Rural laborers	420.1
Total	567.4

By the end of 1991, this figure had grown to 580 million. Earlier in 1980, the total labor force was 420 million and a decade before in 1970 was 340 million. The World Bank forecasts that before the year of 2025, China's total labor force will increase annually by 1.3 percent. According to a report in the *People's Daily*, May 4, 1992, the Chinese government will have to find jobs for 3.6 million urban residents and 100 million rural residents. In 1990, 3.8 million urban residents or 2.6 percent of the total urban labor force had no jobs. The officially announced unemployment rate in 1980 was 4.9 percent, but the figure dropped to about 3 percent in 1984. These figures did not include those who are employed but really have no work, or not enough work to do.

Investigations suggest state enterprises usually employ a work force 15 to 20 percent more than they actually need. Besides, some 100 to 150 million rural laborers are not fully employed. Only a small percentage of rural laborers can obtain urban resident cards and become official urban residents. In the past few years, however, there does exist a floating population in cities, towns and rural areas. In 1990, state enterprises in towns and cities employed some three million contract laborers from the countryside. The development of rural enterprises have also employed a large number of rural workers. Whereas 2.8 million rural laborers worked in rural enterprises in 1978, the figure was 93 million in 1990 when the total production value of rural industry made up 25 percent of the national total. Though working in factories, these contract workers still obtain their land given to them under the responsibility system. Such being the case, 860 million of 1.14 billion Chinese people live in rural areas.

At the same time, we must also realize that state enterprises constitute the mainstay of the Chinese economy. Today, there are some 75,000 state enterprises, 13,000 of which are large and medium-sized. The latter produce half of the total national industrial value and 60 percent of the total profits and taxes collected by the state. Reform in these enterprises is a crucial matter in China's economic reform. The Chinese government is making efforts to solve the "three iron systems": "iron chair"—the guaranteed position for those working in government agencies; "iron rice bowl"—life employment; and "iron salary"—salaries increasing with seniority and totally detached from performance. The government encourages enterprises to make their own wage grades for their workers. The 14th National Congress of the Communist Party of China decided to deepen the reform in state enterprises, which will have a strong impact on the labor force situation. The contract workers system, as a component part of the reform mentioned above, began to be practiced in 1986, when all workers entering state-owned enterprises were hired on a contract basis. Table 2 below shows the 1990 categories of workers in state-owned enterprises. As is shown nearly 14 percent of the total number of workers in these enterprises are contract workers, a percentage still on the rise. Most of these workers have their contracts renewed at the end of the signed period.

Table 2 Workers on the Payroll in State Enterprises (Unit: million)

Regularly employed	77.4
Hired by contract	13.7
Temporary workers	3.5
Others	8.8
Total	103.4

In view of this situation, the State Council issued on July 12, 1986 *Provisional Regulations on Insurance for Workers Waiting for Employment in State-Owned Enterprises,* which went into effect on October 1, 1986. The purpose of these regulations are:

—To support reform of the labor system;
—To promote a rational flow of the labor force;
—To provide basic living expenses for those without jobs;
—To safeguard social stability.

The system of insurance for workers without jobs is a fundamental reform of the past system, under which the jobless were "absorbed" by state-owned enterprises and their subsidiaries in rural areas. For a long time, state-owned enterprises and their rural subsidiaries represented the welfare situation in China. The significance of the reform initiated in 1986, therefore, should be understood from both the conceptual and practical points of view. Traditional forces, however, are very strong in regard to social welfare and to a great degree check the development of insurance for the jobless.

The insurance for the jobless covers workers originally from state-owned enterprises and ensures the livelihood of workers of factories announced bankrupt (or those dismissed as a result of reducing their payroll by enterprises on the verge of bankruptcy), contract workers whose contracts have been terminated or who have been dismissed by the enterprises. Enterprises are requested to turn in 1 percent of the total standard wages of their workers into the fund for insurance of jobless workers, and when the fund falls short of expenses, subsidies are provided by "local" financial

103

CHINA'S SOCIAL SECURITY SYSTEM

departments (the scope of coverage of the insurance system decides which level of local government is to provide the subsidy). Apart from providing relief for the jobless, the fund also supports workers with their medical expenses, vocational training expenses and funds for providing for and helping themselves by going into some kind of production.

Up to now, more than 71 million workers in 440,000 enterprises have entered the unemployment insurance plan. It is estimated that by the end of 1992, the unemployment relief funds had been distributed to more than 420,000 people. Throughout the country, 750 vocational training centers have been established to provide training to more than two million unemployed workers. There are also more than 400 bases to provide workers with opportunities to engage in production for self-relief. These production bases have an annual income of 900 million yuan, and by 1991 had earned 4.25 billion yuan. Each year their spending is about 300 million yuan, and now they have an accumulated fund of more than two billion yuan which has been converted to state bonds, put into bank saving accounts or special accounts of labor departments.

Now, 2,100 unemployment insurance offices have been established by labor departments at the county, prefecture, municipal and provincial levels in the country to oversee management relating to unemployed workers, the rise and spending of unemployment insurance fund, employment guidance and job introduction for the unemployed, organize the unemployed to take part in training for new professions, and help and guide unemployed workers to engage in self-help production or find jobs themselves.

The provisional regulations promulgated by the State Council in 1986 stipulate: those with an employment period of five years or more will get maximum unemployment relief of 24 months, and in the first 12 months the monthly relief is 60 to 75 percent and the second 12 months, 50 percent of their original wages. For those with an employment period of less than five years, relief payment is provided for 12 months with a monthly payment of 60 to 75 percent of their original wages, at a minimum of 50 to 60 yuan, or an average of 65 to 75 yuan. The figure may go up to 76 to 81 yuan if some universal stipends are added. The provisional regulations also stipulate that the following people are not eligible for receiving unemployment relief pay: (1) Their unemployment period has exceeded the prescribed period in which they are eligible for receiving the pay; (2) Those who have been reemployed; (3) Those who have twice refused to accept reemployment without a sound reason; and (4) Those who are being reeducated through forced labor or serving prison terms.

The provisional regulations further stipulate that "Provisional implementation measures should be drawn up by the people's governments of the provinces, autonomous regions and municipalities directly under the Central Government." Therefore, in establishing and implementing unemployment insurance plan, great differences have since occurred among different regions in the scope of unemployment insurance coverage, the source of unemployment insurance funds, the amount, methods of raising and management of the unemployment relief fund.

(2) China has made great headway in its unemployment insurance system, but still leaves much to be desired to meet the requirements of the socialist market economy, which needs emancipation of the mind, change of conception and all-round reforms.

China's current unemployment insurance system started in 1986, with the issuance of *Provisional Regulations on Insurance for Workers Waiting for Employment in State-Owned Enterprises* by the State Council on July 12, 1986. The current system now seems incomplete. First, it has narrow coverage. Secondly, it does not have enough mandatory power, to the extent that over ten percent of the state-owned enterprises have not taken part in it. Thirdly, ways of charges and methods of repayment need further improvement.

The following three questions in China's unemployment insurance system should be solved immediately.

First, who, after all, owns the fund collected for unemployment insurance? This is a question of understanding as well as a question pertinent to our policy and system. The same is true with the current old-age pension plan, the future health security plan and industrial injury insurance. It seems that some people take it as the "state property" or "fund for department concerned." Hence, they try all means possible to turn it into a "bank account" for the mayors or provincial governors, or to take it as part of their revenue. The fund raised by enterprises or individuals for unemployment insurance, or old-age pensions is workers' "money-to-survive," meant to cope with job risks. It is no longer the enterprises' money, nor state property, lest the local or state revenue. Neither is it the money of the department concerned, which only has the responsibility to manage it according to law. Whose money is it, after all? It is the property jointly owned by underwriters of the social security insurance, for which it is solely allocated, but not for embezzlement in any case.

Second, how to handle the surplus saved from unemployment insurance? At present, China has about 2.6 billion yuan of surplus in the unemployment insurance balance. Different people have different views on how to use the money. Some blame departments concerned for inaccurate estimates and overcharging, while others deem the surplus comes from under-repayment. Some criticize it for improper management. All in all, how to view the reproaches and criticisms?

The first criticism is untenable. When the unemployment insurance regulations were worked out, it was estimated that there would be 600,000 unemployed annually and approximately 600 million yuan were needed, which was roughly the same with the annual premium. After the promulgation, the employment situation became serious when it coincided with the three years of streamlining and restructuring. Under "taking stability as the important factor in assessing the whole situation," fewer contract workers terminated contract, while more continued the contract. Directors of enterprises did not dismiss workers who broke rules and regulations because of the situation at the time. There was no more than one case of enterprise bankruptcy. There were only 200,000 unemployed workers in the first four years, with an average of 50,000 per annum, far below the estimated figure. When the situation gradually moved on the normal track in 1991, the number of the unemployed strikingly increased as the labor system was deepening its reform and going for gradual perfection. In 18 months, the unemployed totaled 215,000 people (115,000 in the first six months in 1992), more than the total of the previous four years.

The second criticism should also be analyzed. Is the surplus of 2.6 billion yuan of unemployment insurance expenditure too much? A good answer can only be found through detailed calculation and serious study of the reform situation. In the first place, it is incorrect to think that the unemployment fund only benefits repayment. The unemployment fund in Germany is primarily for job introduction and job training and secondarily for insurance repayment and unemployment relief. They deem it as "positive employment policy." In China, we feel, that in addition to it, we might start labor service enterprises and establish employment bases as well. It is hard to estimate the number of the unemployed. The past estimation was 600,000 unemployed every year, but it turned out to be only 50,000, in one year, 100,000 or 200,000 in another year. This was all before China announced the implementation of a socialist market economy. Will there be any change in the future? At least, it is definite that there will be surplus manpower. But how many in the end? Some say 30 million, while others say 20 or 15 million. After enterprises have the authority on their use of personnel, will the surplus personnel, or part of them, be out of jobs? We advocate for self-digestion by the enterprises as the major measure. And it shouldn't be counted as violation of the principle when enterprises lay off ten percent of the surplus. Take the smallest figure, 15 million for example, ten percent of it means 1.5 million. A relief of 50 yuan per person per month will amount to 900 million yuan a year, much more than the current annual premium. How to correct the situation? How many years can the 2.6 billion yuan cover if the sum is only used for this purpose? Moreover, the current unemployment insurance system needs revision, to meet the new situation of the market economy. It should properly widen its coverage. In principle, it should include all the unemployed and the voluntary unemployed. For instance, will there be unemployment in the state organizations and agencies? How many will be unemployed in the joint venture, collective and private enterprises? In addition to those who fall into the "four categories," how many will it be in the state-owned enterprises? Careful calculation will lead to an appalling figure. It is also necessary to revise the method of repayment. Here are merely three suggestions in face of many necessary revisions: (a) Since the current ways of repayment based on the "standard wage" no longer reflects the work and pay of the workers at the time of their employment, it is suggested to change it into "wage" (including bonus and subsidies in addition to standard wage). Another suggested plan is to delink insurance repayment from one's job payment. For instance, the state stipulates that any unemployed person be given a certain sum of money (50 yuan per month for an example). Though this might be easy to operate, it is unreasonable. Since the social security plan is to spread out "job" risks, the repayment had better not be separated from job payment, but properly reflects the job one has performed. (b) It is suggested to increase the repayment and set a minimum. According to current regulations, the unemployment relief accounts for 60 to 75 percent of the standard wage, which consists of about 56 percent of the "wage," and the relief is 34 to 43 percent of the "wages." When it comes down to exact figures, surveys find that the average monthly unemployment relief payment is around 40 yuan, 10 yuan less than the 50 yuan hard-life line for subsidies (in big cities). Therefore, the repayment should be increased. Naturally, the increment should not be too big, but be kept conducive to the unemployed looking for jobs. Moreover, a minimum should be set, say, 50 yuan per month. (c) Set a waiting period. More than half of the 40-odd countries that have established unemployment insurance system have stipulations on waiting period, 10 days in general, with 2 days as the shortest and 2 months as the longest. Without any stipulations on it, China seems to provide repayments as soon as anyone registers unemployed. This increases the expenditure as much as the workload.

No matter how we expand the coverage or revise the methods

of repayment, they are all to increase the expenditure. So we cannot simply say the sum of 2.6 billion yuan is "much," to say nothing of spending all of it. But we have to make a proper management of it, to cope with possible unemployment problems in the market economy.

The third criticism blames improper management, to be specific, they mean the deposited money, if not put into use, will devalue with the inflation. There is something in it, but no one has found an ideal way out. The best way is to abandon or reduce fees so as to lessen the enterprises' burden. But can this determination be made? Another good idea is that the money is handed to the financial department for investment projects or balancing the financial deficit. This will be in great favor of the nation's construction. Generally speaking, nobody is ready to make the determination. When one or two million people become unemployed under the market economy and the fund is already used up, will the state be able to provide 900 million or 1 billion yuan in a year for unemployment relief? Will the state be able to appropriate funds for the establishment of employment bases?

Third, how should the unemployment insurance affairs be managed, and who should run it? It is correct that the legislative organizations should be separated from executive ones. But how to understand it? Strictly speaking, any administrative department is not a "legislative body." It will be in the correct line so long as the National People's Congress, or its Standing Committee, is not given authority to run social security insurance. Of course, it is inappropriate for the authoritative department to take the fees as well as distribute the money. One way to change the situation is to establish a subordinate institution in charge of the monetary matters. Some say that it will not do if the institution is subordinate to department A (which is in charge of the matter) and it is true "separation of the legislative and executive" only when it is subordinate to department B. This is wrong. How could it be an authoritative department if it does not know how much to charge and distribute? How could department B that is not responsible for the policy-making know how much to charge and distribute?

It is quite amazing that China, as a developing country, has established an unemployment insurance system. It is suggested to further reform insurance coverage, time limit of entitlement to benefits, ratio of money allocation, relief standard, and managing system and to work out a unified national policy framework.

China's unemployment insurance was put into effect only in 1986, but great progress has been made. Now the unemployment insurance is playing an important role socially and economically. But the unemployment insurance system must be strengthened and lots of work must be done. Many localities and departments have explicit plans for reform and, their reforms have far exceeded the scope laid out in unemployment insurance system in 1986. Now it is necessary to consolidate achievements and work out a unified national policy framework to further develop unemployment insurance system.

The types of enterprises covered by the unemployment insurance system varies greatly among different localities. Its general coverage has been extended to state-owned enterprises and large collective-owned enterprises, and it should be extended to all other enterprises, such as all the collective-owned enterprises, joint ventures, township-owned enterprises, private enterprises and other (possibly) self-employed workers and persons.

In the on-the-spot surveys, it is often suggested that unemployment insurance should cover all unemployed workers, no matter what jobs they have, or for whatever reason they have lost their jobs. It is necessary to emphasize that unemployment insurance plans mainly take care of the involuntary unemployed. It is too far out of reason when some often request that unemployment insurance cover the "discipline-violators" who become unemployed mainly on their own account. One way to deal with the situation is to have a stipulation on penalty and limitations in the unemployment insurance, for instance, to postpone the entitlement to relief (6 weeks for an example). This may help them enhance their understanding of reciprocity, that is, workers are entitled to relief and shoulder duties. The malfeasance that deprives one of his entitlement to unemployment relief includes larceny, fraud, drug-smoking, deliberate violations of rules and regulations, frequent absences from work without permission or good reason, habitual disobedience of working hours and repeated dereliction. International Labor Organization's Convention No. 102, Social Security (Minimum Standards), 1952 and convention No. 168, Promotion of Employment and Protection of Unemployment, 1988 stipulate the contingency coverage shall include suspension of earnings due to inability to obtain suitable employment in the case of a person protected who is capable of, and available for, work. The conventions have stipulations on the benefits to which a person protected would otherwise be entitled may be suspended, including:

—where the contingency has been caused by the willful misconduct of the person concerned;

—where the person concerned has lost employment as a direct result of a stoppage of work due to a trade dispute, or has left it voluntarily without just cause;

—where the person concerned has made a fraudulent claim;

—where the person concerned, without just cause, failed to make use of employment services, job guidance, job training, training for a different job and rearrangement of a suitable job.

It is necessary to judge whether an unemployed worker is a true member of the work force and not involuntarily unemployed. This involves the thorny judgment and complicated situations. It is no easy task to differentiate voluntary from involuntary, which often relies on legal procedures and administrative measures before the worker's resignation is clarified whether it is justified or not. In the items mentioned above, particularly to judge whether a worker has the ability to work, employment agency (labor service companies or employment administration) will play a key role.

Therefore, unemployment insurance usually covers those who become unemployed involuntarily from a job with pay. Self-employed, temporary workers and seasonal and agricultural workers are often not included in unemployment insurance (or particularly defined as necessary), so as to avoid management difficulties in registration, money-raising allocations and fixation of income. Workers with a very stable job (as staff in government agencies) sometimes are not included.

China's unemployment insurance plan provides no cover to the new recruits into the work force (such as school graduates). This is expected to continue.

Countries over the world vary greatly in defining maximum period for unemployment relief. Some do not have a maximum period, while some have stipulations of a unified period for all, and still some others combine the period with the fund one raised in the past and years of employment in the past. Exceptional regulations are often made for the relief-receiving period according to different ages and family responsibilities.

The maximum period in China is two years, and it is obviously senseless in view of China's current economy.

Most unemployment insurance systems have stipulations on the initial period from the starting date of unemployment to the date of receiving relief. International Labor Organization's Convention No. 102 allows for a waiting period as long as seven days, mainly to lessen the workload and financial burden of the administrative agencies in handling the fast and frequent occurrences of unemployment. China does not have such a stipulation in its unemployment insurance.

Unemployment risks can not be effectively handled by a single enterprise, but should be extensively spread out to and shared by all the individuals and enterprises that the unemployment insurance covers. China is correct in "universally raising" and "socializing" the unemployment fund, and it should expand it, as extensively as possible, beyond geographical and administrative boundaries, beyond the types and categories of enterprises and workers. It should include all kinds of enterprises and all types of workers. It should go beyond particularly state-owned and collective enterprises and extend to joint ventures, township and private enterprises. When it goes to township enterprises, it actually includes rural and other workers in these enterprises, which is conducive to the circulation of labor force and increasing unemployment funds. Universal fund-raising in cities at the provincial level should be put into practice as soon as possible, then followed by nation-wide universal fund-raising.

The ratio of fund allocations should be based on the total volume of the wages of workers rather than the "standard wage" in the current unemployment insurance system. This will consolidate the foundation for China's unemployment insurance system, which will, in the future, play an important and comprehensive role in worker welfare.

The mandatory one percent has already brought about revenue far more than the necessary expenditure, the annual revenue of 900 million yuan over 300 million yuan expenses. But the investment opportunities for good end-result from the accumulated fund are very limited. The accumulated fund earns low interest when it is deposited in banks, or used to buy state bonds. The fund must be used for short term investment with high yield. It is reported that the managerial expenses is 5 to 8 percent of the fund (in some provinces it is as high as 25 percent). Great efforts should be made to bring down the percentage to 3 to 5 percent.

The relief standard is 60 to 75 percent of the standard wage, which is about 60 percent of an individual's total wage, therefore, the relief is between 36 and 45 percent of the total average wage. The International Labor Organization's Convention No. 102 (Minimum Standards), 1952 points out that 45 percent of the average income is the ideal basic percentage for unemployment relief. China's unemployment insurance system matches the convention in this respect. But it should take into consideration China's low wage, just enough to cover the daily necessity expenses. Most of the workers in cities and towns rely on subsidies such as housing. This shows that the traditional prevailing position of the state-owned enterprises will continue to exist.

Another question related to the relief fund is the concept of "standard wage" in calculating the relief standards (and allocation ratio). It seems more appropriate to replace it with the total wage of workers. In the discussions during the survey, it was suggested that 75 percent of the total wage of workers to be taken as the national unified relief standard is fairly appropriate.

The adjustment of relief standards, including minimum standards, is temporary and only reflects major changes in price and wage. It is suggested to regulate adjustment of relief standards (once in a year, for example), only to reflect changes in the retail price index. This is extremely important to whether the unemployment insurance plans can keep going, and whether the living standard of the workers can be guaranteed.

Regarding management, the goal of social security includes: serving the customers (to provide customers with high quality service such as fair, polite and proficient service all the time); support from the staff (provide a fine working environment so that the work done by the staff is satisfactory); quality (timely distribution with the quality as usual); creative (encourage new ideas to push forward necessary improvements for better service); responsibility to explain (to explain the distributed fund so as to keep social security plans consistent).

China has a very short history of social security plans with management as the main problem. In the past, management totally fell in the hands of the administrative organizations of the state-owned enterprises. Many questions need be resolved, including: to work out new and unified laws as well as a series of regulations and decrees on social security; to introduce proficient ways of filing individuals' and enterprises' records such as establishing a computer system; to establish information systems to provide important data for decision-making, managing and accounting; to set up training centers for social security and carry out the training plans for decision-makers and administrators; to work out explicit regulations for customers to appeal, and systematic procedures to review pensions and relief; to work out and carry out auditing programs, particularly the auditing programs on management expenses; to unfold publicity drives to let the whole society (particularly the workers) understand the role that the social security relief fund plays now and in the future.

It is crucial that the unemployment insurance plans should be conducive to the nation's economic reform and restructuring. Unemployment insurance plans should be aimed at involuntarily unemployed workers, and encourage them to be reemployed as soon as possible and accept training. It should be supplementary to the more extensive employment training, education and restructuring. It is highly necessary to emphasize the importance of being reemployed after training. Unemployment insurance plans should support training activities within the limit of its resources. Henceforth, it is urgently necessary to establish sound and proficient employment services so as to help the labor force market operate and ensure their coordination with relief fund distribution centers. It is imperative to have a concordant way to handle security of workers' income and labor market planning.

It is necessary to enthusiastically encourage the establishment and development of the above mentioned institutions, to ensure the implementation of the policy for employment promotion. It is necessary to reinforce their function as employment agencies, to make up for what is missing, and help the circulation of the labor force.

Through "self-help company for production," these agencies actually engage in enterprising activities, directly sharing the subsidies for the surplus man power from state-owned enterprises. This is an embodiment of the problem of the gigantic surplus labor force, the necessity of "maintaining social stability" and the typical past theory of "absorption." Nevertheless, it is totally undesirable for these agencies to be directly involved in low efficiency production activities (which are protected by taxation reduction).

Conclusion: In the past ten to fifteen years, the labor market in many countries is deteriorating with the unemployment figure, long-term unemployment in particular, rising drastically. Many countries, therefore, have made major revisions of their unemployment insurance plans, and this has resulted in a more complicated situation. Some countries shortened the period of relief that one was entitled to, and added more limitations to distribution, while some other countries raised the relief standard for certain groups (like the old-aged workers), prolonged the period for relief that one was entitled to and the increment of the expenses, usually came from government appropriations. It is extraordinary for China, whose economy is in a developing stage, to have established unemployment insurance system. Up to now, people are restrained in their unemployment insurance requests

CHINA'S SOCIAL SECURITY SYSTEM

and they have to take a cautious attitude towards its future development. It is suggested mainly to expand coverage for various kinds of enterprises and increase the fund allocation at higher levels in the initial developing stage. The coverage of unemployment insurance should focus on involuntarily unemployed workers who need income protection during their active search for jobs. It is inadvisable to provide unlimited security for all unemployed workers. The relief fund allocation for the unemployment insurance should be related to the average total wage rather than the average standard wage. The combination of relief fund with retail price index will vitalize the unemployment insurance system.

It needs to be pointed out that unemployment insurance plans will play a positive role in China's economic reform. The unemployment insurance plans will protect the life of workers who lose jobs temporarily, enhance the efficiency of enterprises and promote the circulation of the labor force. Nevertheless, the unemployment insurance plan will not solve the fundamental problem of the restructuring of the economic structure. It must be closely combined with other plans and reform measures, particularly those pertinent to the labor market.

The key to perfect the unemployment insurance plans lies in the emancipation of mind, change of conception and foster among the workers in cities and towns and the vast youths new ideas of the labor system that is in line with the socialist market economy.

It is more than six years now since the State Council issued the *Provisional Regulations on Insurance for Workers Waiting for Employment in State-Owned Enterprises.* In the first four years, 200,000 people received unemployment relief, but 200,000 people in 1991 alone and 115,000 people in the first six months of 1992. Gradual increase was the trend and the general developing speed was quite slow. The situation that enterprises had abundant surplus labor force was not changed much. It naturally had something to do with the small coverage of the current unemployment insurance plans, and the lack of experience in implementation. But what limited the pushing of the plans mainly stemmed from the old labor and payment system, its ideological concept and public opinion.

Shortly after the founding of the People's Republic of China, China faced a situation of 23.6 percent unemployment rate left over from old China. It adopted a policy of enthusiastic restoration of production, distributing relief to and re-employing the unemployed, and taking in all the staff in the public and educational institutions of the old regime, and all the workers of the bureaucratic capitalist enterprises. Under the slogan of "a meal for three should be shared by five," it was strictly prohibited to dismiss workers and fixing employment and unifying assignment of jobs was taken as the main task of democratic refrom. It was entirely correct to take the emergency measures, which played a positive role at that time. In 1957, when the first Five-year Plan was accomplished, the short-comings of the rigid and highly concentrated labor system began to show up. Noticing it, the Central Government immediately put forward the idea of two education systems and two labor systems, and demanded reduction rather than increase of the number of "fixed workers." For various reasons, the reform of the labor system was given up halfway and this helped to distort the concept and foster traditional habits, to cause more difficulties for reform.

It is imperative to change the concept that the labor force "belongs to the state or public" into one that it is possessed by the laborer himself. In the past highly concentrated planning economy with unified employment and assignment, people often said that once you got through the public institutions' doorsteps you became a man of the state. In fact, it was not a socialist idea nor did it conform to Marxist basic theory, but somehow it, in practice, became the source of eating in the state's "big rice squadron" and "iron rice bowl." Socialism should provide laborers with more choices of jobs than capitalism, so as to create better conditions for the rational circulation of the laborers and the full play of their talents, wisdom and enterprising spirit. This means that it is important to recognize the laborers' right of self-determination.

It is imperative to change the concept of the main body over employment and life-long fixed employment. Under the socialist market economy, the government should no longer play the role as the main body over employment while only the enterprises are the main body over employment. Workers, technicians and managers are all "staff of the enterprise" rather than "staff of the state," as they were called in the past. The government will no longer have universal recruitment, assignment and management. Enterprises have the authority to recruit and dismiss workers. Workers have the right to choose jobs. The relationship between the employer and the employee is set through labor laws and contract. This is not in contradiction of workers as the masters, which will be embodied chiefly through the right and duty of the citizen. It is essential to do away with the concept of life-long, fixed employment, and develop the concept of market mechanism and labor market all over the society, in order to revitalize enterprises and increase productivity and economic end-results. It is possible for any worker, including those in public service, to be dismissed or have employment terminated. Everybody should have a sense for crisis and emergency. Public opinion should turn to recognize that the termination of employment and dismissal is normal, but should not assume someone must be wrong when he or she is dismissed or has employment terminated. It is equally necessary to protect the safety of the owner of the enterprise. The sense for crisis and emergency, which encourages workers to do their best in their work, does not contravene the relative stability of the workers, which means to attract the workers with the enterprise's business achievement from departure.

Besides the change of concept, we should also reform the distribution system. In state-owned enterprises, wage is only part of a worker's income. This involves the question of distribution. Besides wages, workers now have benefits such as housing, pensions, medical care, price subsidies, etc. It is imperative to make the distribution system conform with the new mechanism for the establishment of the socialist market economy. It is important to gradually use less and less of the past distribution system of free supply, give the wage a bigger percentage and make the distribution system more transparent. Reform, including price reform, is the natural trend.

The use of the unemployment insurance fund should follow the principles of "proper collection" and "proficient utilization." The former means to fix a proper fund collection ratio for enterprises and control over-accumulation of funds and an unnecessary increase in burdens on enterprises in line with the labor system reform and unemployment rate. The latter means the use of the fund should be legalized, regularized and put under a strict responsibility system to avoid the loss and transfer of the fund.

Should the relief fund be collected from enterprises, or from both the enterprises and workers? This deserves study before a final conclusion is drawn. It has strong points in letting workers share certain responsibilities, but it is impractical if workers shoulder too much responsibility because of the low wage system in China. China should go in the direction that workers share part of it, even if it is a tiny part, when their wages increase by a large margin.

China's current unemployment insurance provides a longer period of relief than some developed countries. The United States has a six month-period of relief in general, at most nine months if it is extended for three months. China has a twenty-four-month-period for its low wage system and being not so easy to find new jobs after unemployment as in developed countries. All in all, China should adhere to the principle that "it should favor protecting the unemployed in their basic living, as well as encouraging them to find new jobs, in order to mobilize their enthusiasm for employment and prevent them from relying on state relief.

2. Problems in Drafting the Reform Plan

(1) China's reform in unemployment insurance should go in for the establishment of one of its own by drawing fine practices and successful experiences from foreign countries, as well as taking into full consideration China's reality.

How to find the road? The theory by the Nobel Prize laureate Professor Ronald Coase might be of some help. According to his theory, unemployment is considered a kind of contamination. That the loss caused by unemployment of the staff increases social costs, is an "externalized diseconomy." Then how to solve the "externalized diseconomy?" The traditional way is that the government levies tax on enterprises to compensate the unemployed for their losses. Is this the most economical method? Obviously not. There are two ways to solve the problem of unemployment: one is to compensate the unemployed for their loss, who are to wait in the society, and the other is to lower wages to enable enterprises to employ more people. Which is more economic? The most economic method can only be found through the selection of the market. The result might be the following: as far as the best labor market is concerned, made up of big enterprises, probably the most economic method to solve the unemployment problem is to increase employment by cutting wages and training in the enterprises. This has been borne out by the Japanese system like "life-long employment." In the second-rate labor market made up of small enterprises, a quite economic way perhaps is to let the unemployed go by giving them a certain amount of economic compensation. But how to accomplish the selection? That is where the government's role lies, according to Professor Coase, so long as the defining of authority is accurate and reasonable, the selection through market must be the most economic. Then, how to define the government's authority? It will rely on the comparison of operational costs. If the enterprise is to solve the unemployment problem through increasing employment by cutting wages, it is better to let the enterprise have the authority because it costs less for it to decide whether to dismiss workers or to increase employment by cutting wages. If a trade union is to make the decision, the cost will be gigantic because it will be very difficult for workers to reach, among themselves, a low wage agreement, which is also acceptable for the employers. On the contrary, it will cost the least when the responsibility goes to workers themselves if it is to decide to dismiss workers with certain compensation. Should China establish such a social security system? In terms of mandatory insurance, big enterprises may carry out the following plan: The government establishes an autonomous foundation whose fund is raised by big enterprises. What is the rate? It is suggested to use the American method of empirical premiums rate. It is at the disposal of the enterprises to choose to increase or decrease dismissal. If it is to increase, then it will pay more premiums and if it is to decrease, it will pay lower ones. Small enterprises, in whatever economic sector may implement the following plan: Employees themselves establish such foundation that employers and employees consult to choose whether to enter into the plan for big enterprises or the one for small ones. And the problems of long-time unemployment and the large number unemployment caused by intense economic fluctuations should be solved through government relief because neither enterprises nor workers can bear the responsibility. Tax-exemptions and relief by government should be used to encourage the establishment of autonomous insurance systems, including severance pay given by enterprises or co-ops organized by workers themselves, along with mandatory insurance.

On the question of solving the problem of on-the-job unemployment. An important background when China put forward unemployment insurance is to relieve abundant surplus personnel, and to overcome the social tremor that the drive for efficiency may bring about. It is futile by only relying on unemployment relief without other measures to solve the tremendous problem of on-the-job unemployment. There isn't a single solution to the problem. Hence, the major approach is to mobilize funds and develop production. About a dozen years ago, there was an unbelievable reform in labor and wages when the employment policy of "three combinations" was put forward in 1982. Its positive significance was that for the first time China recognized the right of workers to get organized or become self-employed.

Apart from this, attention should also be paid to the permission of moonlighting. The negative side is that in some enterprises almost everybody goes in for moonlighting to make more money at the expenses of the primary job. The positive side is that many people earn much more than their primary job pay. Can they be disconnected from, or leave, the state-owned enterprises at an appropriate time? In fact, it provides a new approach or transitional method to tackle on-the-job unemployment in state-owned enterprises. These are the most important ones. In the end, the unemployment problem in economically developed areas might be easy to settle while that in economically backward regions remains a hard nut to crack, particularly difficult for state-owned enterprises. Labor forces should be encouraged to move about. Some people have prejudice against the migration of farmers from under-developed areas to developed areas. The flow has a positive significance. Without migration, rich villages like Daqiuzhuang of Tianjin and Muping of Shandong would never find their way out. It is equally true with township enterprises in Jiangsu and Zhejiang provinces. A long-term unemployment insurance plan for the on-the-job unemployed after the circulation may be established in accordance with the market economy.

(2) Drafting the plan: to define the liability shared by enterprises and workers; to define the legal liability of any individual worker; expand the coverage of unemployment insurance.

International specialists believe that China's social security reform mainly refers to unemployment insurance, whose purpose is: first, enterprises enjoy greater authority in promoting the circulation of the labor force so as to ensure that every enterprise will contribute to compensation for accidental loss; secondly, to alleviate the social impact caused by the enhancement of responsibility of the workers in economic reform. If these goals can be achieved, it means that all the problems in the following three respects are solved.

First, the additional responsibility of the enterprises. The protection of social unemployment through social security means that enterprises' direct responsibility for employment is changed into an indirect and additional one, and it is only to raise fund for unemployment, or to promote employment. However, the question is: does the reform mean that enterprises are the only resource for unemployment funds?

The past practice of life-long security of employment explains why enterprises were the only contributors to the unemployment insurance fund in China. No doubt, it was factories' responsibility to compensate for industrial accidents. But should the security of employment be regarded as another responsibility of the enterprises? They do not deserve it. In the United States, the premium each employer pays varies according to the unemployment rate of the enterprise. Because the unemployment problem involves factors external to enterprise, it is not accepted across the board. What's more, in some other countries, employers pay a universal premium, and in some countries, only the employers pay the premium. In most countries, at least two parties contribute to the fund, with the employers providing more than the employees, even if the state is not the third contributor. Here is a proposal therefrom: Workers themselves need to pay a certain sum of premium because the increase of unemployment figure increases spending on unemployment insurance compensation. Undoubtedly, it would be very difficult to get along if the wage does not have a corresponding increment. And branch institutions of social security should keep pace with it in the compensation dealings among enterprises.

Second, responsibility of an individual worker. The maximum period for compensation is determined by a worker's years of employment, though he or she does not share the insurance expenses. There are several traditional reasons that a worker contributes to insurance fund: money needed for contingency; the party that is entitled to compensation is opposed to the delegation of the right to dispose; workers take part in insurance management through their representatives. They would like to limit the insurance expenses. These are mainly psychological factors. Even though workers do not contribute to the fund in economic terms, the contribution by employers may be generally deemed as part of the workers' payment.

If a worker has the responsibility, particularly the responsibility that he or she must accept the job offered by employment services, it is necessary to keep the responsibility within legal measures. Should there be limitations in the situations such as resignation, or accepting relief for short-period unemployment after repeated refusal of offers for jobs? Should there be distinctions in accordance with international standards if the job offered for a worker is regarded as suitable? In many countries, many things, such as the worker's age, years of employment, work experience and whether it is convenient for him to go to and from his new job, have to be considered before it is deemed suitable. Usually there should be proper arbitration or appeal before ruling, as in solving disputes between employer and employee.

Third, the expansion of unemployment insurance services. Will the unemployment insurance services keep within a certain limitation, as they are currently limited to the state-owned enterprises, without expanding the scope of service, to say nothing of including private and collective enterprises when socialized market economy is established? Out of different considerations, private, joint venture and state-owned enterprises have to contemplate the need of unemployment risks and employment protection. The expansion of insurance coverage is economically reasonable because free and fair competition among different enterprises needs to have equal labor costs. Undoubtedly, it is imperative to take administrative mandatory measures to carry out the plan, just as implementing other social security plans. Of course, those enterprises whose number of employees is below the minimum standards, probably will not be covered by the plan, and it is at least so during the transitional period.

If the liability of both the enterprises and the workers is explicitly defined in the unemployment insurance plan, it is important for the promotion of the change into socialized market economy to recognize their joint liability, and to permit the combination of their representatives and government representatives to take part in unemployment insurance plans and employment services.

(3) On voluntary unemployment insurance

The form of unemployment insurance may vary. Besides mandatory insurance, there is, in the world, voluntary insurance supported by government, unemployment subsidies encouraged by government, saving-like unemployment insurance, so on and so forth. Then should China establish voluntary unemployment insurance? There are different views worlds apart.

One view is: it is imperative to encourage the establishment of voluntary insurance.

Some feel that government encouragement and provision of services to push the application of voluntary unemployment insurance in China has some connections with learning from newly industrialized countries or regions. It has some foundation in China because China has a tradition of co-operative insurance, primarily in rural areas. This tradition may come in use. Voluntary insurance in Europe is based on trade unions, which is inconvenient for China. It is an excellent approach for employees to set up voluntary insurance in co-operative ways with governmental encouragement and assistance. This also includes supplementary insurance provided by employers, who may enter into mandatory insurance as well as supplementary insurance, if they feel it is econmically rational. For instance, when they need to dismiss workers, they may choose to give more severance pay on the basis of mandatory insurance. The Chinese people have a tradition in doing this. Moreover, it also includes commercial unemployment insurance started by companies. The commercial one may play a positive role under sound legal regulations.

Voluntary insurance is supplementary to, rather than a total dependent of mandatory insurance. This has been proved in European countries.

Another view is: voluntary insurance is unsuccessful and impractical at present.

It was a success only in the past when the state gave large subsidies to encourage everybody to take part in it. Otherwise, those who took part in it would bear too big a risk when returns fell short of contributions. Now some Scandinavian countries adopt the voluntary method because a high percentage of trade union members enter into it. But we should not neglect that there is government plan to compensate those who voluntarily enter into unemployment insurance in Sweden and Finland. As a matter of fact, it becomes a government plan for everybody.

Social security should have an element of compulsion. China's constitution clearly stipulates that it is not only the citizen's right but also duty to enter into insurance. If it is voluntary, not only the unemployment risk will not be protected, but it will check the progress of reform. As voluntary insurance is separated from the mandatory type, it will inevitably bind the circulation of the labor force. If we are determined to establish a market economy, we should pay attention to other countries' lessons. It is suggested to put aside voluntary insurance in the field of social security, because it is impossible for unemployment insurance to get developed overnight. Voluntary insurance should be encouraged, instead of being objected, in places with no unemployment insurance.

Some point out that commercial insurance is unfeasible as voluntary unemployment insurance to ensure economic development of the whole country. That the P.B.G.C. in the United States may soon fall apart is a case in point. The risk will be huge if it is voluntary contribution.

At present it is inappropriate for China's unemployment plan to push for individual contributions. There are two problems in it. One is the understanding of social security while the other is financial resources. It is too soon to enhance workers' understanding by requesting them to pay because Chinese workers are not mentally prepared for unemployment. Moreover, the low wage practice constitutes no financial resource. Of course this does not mean we should never develop individual contributions, because everything is changing in these aspects.

Still another view is: China's unemployment insurance may take more approaches and the voluntary one is supplementary to the mandatory.

China's unemployment insurance system is at an initial stage, covering only four categories of people. There is a course of development if the coverage is to be enlarged. A cautious attitude is needed if the 90 million workers of township-run enterprises are to be included in the plan. Under this situation, more forms of insurance, rather than only a mandatory one, will be under exploration.

Unemployment insurance plans of a higher standard may be considered. Nevertheless, there should be a principle, that is, not to impose a heavy burden on enterprises, and not to collect more fees from them. Old-age pension plans may have various kinds. For instance, besides the basic mandatory old-age pension, there will be a supplementary old-age pension and savings account. The supplementary one should be voluntary and based on the enterprises' economic achievements. A nationwide uniformed pension will not do. The same is true with unemployment insurance. If some enterprises or individuals, such as township-run enterprises, are willing to enter into voluntary insurance plans, they may have it as a supplement to the mandatory one without increasing the enterprises' burden. China's current labor cost is less than 10 percent of the production value, not high in terms of wage but not low in general as it seems. Low labor costs is China's forte. So an old-age pension unemployment insurance plan should be based on the control or gradual deduction of the enterprises' labor costs, so as to help the economy develop with a higher competitiveness.

3. The Combination of Unemployment Insurance and Employment Services

(1) The key for the combination of unemployment insurance and employment services suitable for China lies in the internal digestion within the enterprises and bringing into play labor service companies.

Digestion within the enterprises is the key in handling surplus personnel.

One task in establishing a socialist market economy is to change the situation of "a meal for three shared by five," "making three-men's work a job for five," to strive for higher economic achievement. This is the only way out for enterprises to march toward the market. What is the employment situation that China faces? China sees approximately fifteen million new workers each year. Six to seven million people, both newly grown-ups and rural labor force flowing into cities, need jobs in cities or towns. There are seventy million workers in state-run enterprises, and the figure reaches 100 million if workers in government institutions are counted. Of this gigantic workforce, 15, 20, or 25 percent are surplus personnel, roughly fifteen million. How to solve the contradiction between increasing efficiency and handling surplus personnel? The fundamental and positive way is to develop the economy. Next comes the development of tertiary industry. There are two other problems to be tackled. One is how to solve the problem of laborers flowing into urban areas. The flowing of rural laborers into cities should be controlled at an appropriate level. At present, China has 1.4 billion *mu* (Six *mu* equals an acre.) of cultivated land with 300 million rural workers. If one worker takes care of 10 *mu*, it needs 100 million workers, so it is not overestimated to say 200 million are surplus rural workers. Cities and towns could never stand it if rural workers are flooding into urban areas at will. The policy should be to encourage farmers to leave the farmland, instead of the homeland, to find jobs in township-run enterprises or tertiary industries or other production fields in rural areas. The other is the arrangement of surplus workers in urban enterprises. If the 15-million-strong surplus workers are pushed to the society, it would cause stability problems. Some of them may leave enterprises and go to the society, or turn to unemployment security institutions to be trained for new jobs. But the figure could not, and should not, be very big.

China could not, and should not see tens of millions of unemployed workers, for it might easily cause social instability. Hence, the arrangement of surplus personnel should only follow the principle of "taking the digestion within the enterprise as the main with social adjustment as the auxiliary approach," to combine vocational training and on-the-job training with enhancing workers' quality. The major part of the unemployment fund should be used in job training instead of relief to solve the unemployment problem. Do workers in enterprises have the desire for training? Absolutely positive. The middle-aged workers in their thirties are the backbone of enterprises, at the same time they grew up during the ten years of turmoil of the "Cultural

Revolution." They were victims in cultural and technical studies, but they have a strong desire for knowledge. Some enterprises have this practice: if it is a three-shift production, the enterprise organizes four shifts to rotate with the extra one having a special time of cultural and technological study. If it is a two-shift it arranges three shifts. By doing so, it improves the quality of its staff through the rotation of training. The difficulty is how to combine internal digestion and training with unemployment insurance institutions. The institutions should, with a positive attitude, coordinate with leaders of the enterprise in training surplus personnel inside and outside the enterprise. Training for a new job as one of the important tasks of the institutions helps solve the employment problem of the surplus personnel, as well as promote the enhancement of the quality of workers. This is the right combination of unemployment security with resolution of surplus personnel that fits China's reality.

There are some problems in labor service companies, and running them by administrative means is the major one.

Some specialists are for the combination of positive employment policy with unemployment security. Part of the unemployment fund might be earmarked for training. Employment services might be combined with unemployment insurance plans. There is quite a long waiting period before an unemployed person gets relief. The waiting period, not merely for the examination of qualification, has an important function of helping the foundation and the workers in their utmost efforts to find suitable jobs before they obtain relief. Then comes the expansion of employment, self-relief production as it is called in China. China may continue to use part of the unemployment fund, plus employment fund of the past, to start an enterprise that takes in large numbers of youths for their first jobs.

What are the problems in combining unemployment relief with employment promotion? It is achieved mainly through labor service companies, which shoulder the administrative responsibility of providing employment and job training as much as running factories and shops. They have played a very positive role in employment. Nevertheless, there are quite a few problems. In the first place, the training done entirely by labor service companies, means nothing but administration-organized training without the mechanism of choice. The unemployment training cannot be the most economical one, but often causes wastes and makes the structure irrational. Should the enterprise, combining the insurance fund with the training fund, choose to dismiss more and distribute more relief or dismiss fewer and use the money for on-the-job training? The enterprise can have the most economical and appropriate training by making the decision based on market information. The biggest problem of China's labor service companies is running the enterprise with administrative methods. They turn out to be neither a civil affairs institution, nor an enterprise. Except a few with good economic effect, most of the companies throughout the nation cannot make both ends meet. And some inefficient doings have popped up. For example, some enterprises turn the labor service companies into their own revenue channel to dodge taxes. China's practice in the past forty years and more has proven that running enterprises in administrative ways is a failure. It makes no difference with workers employed without job in state-run enterprises in the past. The reform should be the separation of the functions of labor service companies, that is, it should be a service agency without running enterprises if it belongs to the government. A share holding system may be practiced by the current labor service companies, to revitalize them by taking the company as the major share holder while attracting capital from others. Then how are these enterprises expected to help solve employment problems? It is suggested to encourage them to take in more laborers by providing them with wage subsidies and reducing taxation.

Specialists believe that labor service companies play a very big role and they should cover the unemployment insurance.

The emergence of "labor service companies" is an achievement of China's reform and opening up policy and a pioneering action in solving the employment problem. A case in point is that these companies employed or temporarily employed 8.7 million people at the end of 1991. Now there are a total of 36,000 labor service companies running 410,000 enterprises or workshops with a total production value of 108.6 billion yuan. These companies can be divided into two categories, ones run by labor departments and others run by other departments or enterprises. The former have four functions: first, employment introduction; second, employment training; third, unemployment insurance; fourth, running labor service companies. And the State Council began to call the latter labor service enterprises.

Unemployment insurance is a component part of the social security system, and is also an important part of the employment service system in terms of employment services, because the fuctions of job introduction, job training, unemployment insurance and running enterprises all serve to resolve employment problems. They are inter-related, mutually complementary and none is dispensable. So it is highly necessary to contemplate how to perfect the employment service system when China is improving and perfecting its unemployment insurance system. Some of Germany's experiences may be drawn. The unemployment insurance fund is set up from the insurance premium. Two-thirds of the fund is used for job introduction, employment training and establishing necessary labor service enterprises or bases of self-relief production. And less than one third goes to relief distribution.

(2) It is imperative to establish an unemployment insurance system with supply as its core.

Experts believe that social security can play a positive role in preventing unemployment and promoting employment.

The social security system may be designed as a three-layer system. The legalized part is the first layer, while the employment plan is the second. The fixation of a basic wage figure may serve as the guiding line that premium will be collected at a certain rate on that part of the wage and the money collected will be taken as financial support for the legalized part. In some countries, there isn't such a regulation. The fixation of a basic figure has an important impact on employment: first, it stimulates enterprises to use fewer workers and encourages them to prolong working hours, but not to recruit more workers; second, the premium rate is relatively higher than in those situations that do not have a fixation of basic figure, therefore, it increases the cost of unskilled workers and restricts the employment of new workers in labor intensive enterprises.

Unemployment compensation enables enterprises to reorganize production and increase productivity, so as to make themselves adapt to the development of new technology and needs of the market, instead of cutting down the number of workers whose working hours are reduced for the time being. The reason is that enterprises are more willing to let workers work, instead of terminating their contracts.

After the termination of the contract, the worker may receive unemployment relief or a big sum of welfare relief. Nevertheless, either is lower than his past wage. In other countries, the employer who continues to pay or partially pay workers during their unemployment period enjoys unemployment insurance compensation. If the workers do temporary work, the money they earn, or the total money they receive from the so-called partial unemployment, is usually less than the money they earned as full-time workers, but more than the complete-unemployment relief, so that workers whose working hours are reduced won't feel hopeless under the threat of complete unemployment.

For the sake of employment, such solution should be subject to the following:

Temporary unemployment or decreased income because of enterprises' responsibility of unemployment compensation should not be taken as the excuse for keeping surplus workers on the job, but should give enterprises the opportunity to reorganize production or train or re-arrange workers within them. This may indeed cut down the number of workers permanently, for some workers are trained for new jobs while some others are dismissed. This may increase the enterprises' financial burden on unemployment insurance because of the training of workers. This makes enterprises spend production costs on recruiting new workers. If they have to dismiss previous workers, this is the only approach. By doing so, the employer can make experienced workers suitable for the enterprise.

Under specific conditions, it should have the approval from the labor department and unemployment insurance company, which the reorganization and re-training plans of enterprises should follow. They are in a better position to appraise the operation after the reorganization than administrative departments. The termination of employment contracts and temporary reduction of working hours are usually matters for negotiation between enterprises and trade union representatives.

Unemployment insurance is only enjoyed by workers in particular areas, usually in a city, a province or autonomous region in China. If a worker is allowed to move from one area to another, particularly under the situation of employment market at a nationwide level, it is imperative to take co-ordinated measures among various unemployment insurance plans, so that workers are entitled to unemployment insurance payments. In similar situations, other countries usually adopt internal coordination in terms of short-range interests. The competent unemployment insurance department will take into consideration the period of service, or the period of service of a worker under another unemployment insurance plan of the country, so as to ensure that the worker is entitled to insurance payments and make it easy to calculate the welfare pay and determine the maximum period for payments. The problem and its solution is similar to the coordination in giving pensions, except it is simpler.

It is imperative to have a special management channel between the institution specialized in unemployment insurance and that of employment, to oversee the qualification of entitlement to welfare. An unemployed worker must register at an employment department because refusal of a proper job offer and training will lead to suspension, reduction or cancellation of welfare benefit. Anyway, a worker need not go to the labor department for repeated verification but have to look for a job or be trained before he or she has a good chance for a new job.

It is to give financial support to the promotion of employment through unemployment insurance plans. Positive and encouraging support fits unemployed workers and those under the threat of unemployment. Under special conditions, particularly when the region or industry is in a depressed state, the whole procedure of dismissing, training, re-assigning and arranging of surplus workers should go through negotiations between the employer and trade union and have combined employment service with unemployment service, so as to avoid unemployment as much as possible. In some cases, the trainee who left his or her job may receive unemployment relief.

Anyway, the circulation of laborers and the unemployment insurance fund for the unemployed should not be nullified because the state is responsible for providing financial support to personnel assignment and training and should not improperly limit the budget for unemployment compensation.

The most important thing is to provide employment opportunities, instead of unemployment insurance.

In most countries that have an unemployment insurance system, unemployment relief receivers usually have to register at employment agencies. In Hong Kong and some Asian countries, they have to go to the government labor department to look for new jobs. Employment agencies can help reduce the number of relief receivers and the length of time they rely on relief.

The reason why they have to go and register at the labor department or employment agency is that the purpose of unemployment insurance is not to create dependence, but to help the unemployed find new jobs and overcome difficulties. During unemployment, the unemployed can receive re-training and improve skill so that he or she can find a job to use the skill learned. Labor service companies, like employment agencies in other countries, can provide an effective channel for enterprises to choose workers and the latter to choose the former. But the most important thing enabling them to provide effective service is the establishment of a proficient data network, that is, they must master effective information about the labor market. In some countries, the best way is to place labor service companies or employment agencies directly under a government department, as this helps to put all the information together and promotes information exchanges.

Another important factor related to unemployment insurance is re-training and on-the-job training, which are not only conducive to helping the unemployed shake off dependence on relief, but also helps laborers improve their skills. Generally, the training is jointly funded by the government and the unemployed that are insured against unemployment. Occasionally, the government provides subsidies to encourage training. The current unemployment insurance plan in China should provide the unemployed with opportunities and conditions for training. No doubt, it is much better to enable the unemployed to find new jobs than to encourage them to rely on relief. Providing re-training and on-the-job training is a more positive measure than just giving out relief payments.

The planning of re-training and on-the-job training must be consistent with government policy on human resources. Labor departments in China should do their utmost in providing information of what jobs are most wanted and what kind of training benefits the unemployed. In some countries or regions, such as in Singapore, the Republic of Korea and Hong Kong, there is an "employment training society," not only to provide job training for the new laborers to get into the market but also to re-train the unemployed. China should take the good advice, that is, to establish employment training society in every city, and take in representatives from the Labor Ministry, trade unions and other pertinent departments to provide necessary training for the unemployed.

The most important thing to remember is the relationship between unemployment insurance on the one hand, and the improvement of workers' skills and the increase of labor productivity on the other. The establishment of an unemployment insurance system is not merely to guarantee the basic daily necessity of the unemployed during their unemployment, but what is more important is to ensure that they have chances to receive training, find new jobs and improve their skills during the period.

Naturally, the most important thing is not how to distribute relief but to provide opportunities for employment. If there are many job opportunities, it does not matter when one loses his job for a short while. Moreover, if one wants to change his job, he may get the training for it because job training opportunities are provided. If he is leading a difficult life, it means the security plan lacks a guarantee of providing daily necessities. All in all, the experience of the rising developed countries is: Providing employment opportunities, instead of unemployment insurance, is the most important thing.

Supply should be taken as the core of the unemployment security structure.

Experts from the World Bank suggest that generally speaking, unemployment security in China is not an issue of need but an issue of supply. This is a very important view. The issue of supply is, in the final analysis, an issue of structure. Those between thirty to forty years old who grew up during the "Cultural Revolution" need re-training.

Along with more and more high technology, such as electronic devices and telecommunication equipment, used in economic operations, many workers with low skills cannot read operation manuals and do not know how to operate the equipment. In a sense, they will be cast out by the advancement of economy if they are not able to receive re-training. Singapore has established an unemployment insurance system with supply as its core, which is, in practice, a system of training and re-training. It basically includes the following two aspects: (a) The government participates in, to a great extent, and contributes to the technical training fund with large subsidies. The government plays a remedial role when the "market fails." (b) To win support from the employers. First is to guide employers to guarantee the time for training, and next comes asking employers' associations to make employers participate in all kinds of technical training, curriculum designing, for an example. And then promise employers that workers will be more enthusiastic after they have improved their skills through technical training or obtained certain certificates. That is why there is a series of special courses and basic skill training courses such as language and math courses. Video is even used in some training courses. If Chinese men and women in their 30s or early 40s feel that it is losing face to go to school at such an age, they may take the video tape back home. There are other social and cultural factors to be contemplated. The government has made great publicity among those between thirty-five to forty years old. If one receives training, he or she will get promotion or a better job. Twelve years efforts have made initial success without problems in structural unemployment. It is expected to last for another fifteen years, because it involves continuous training of a whole generation till their retirement.

Chapter IV
China's Medical Insurance System

1. Principles of Reform and Basic Problems

(1) The aim and goal of the reform is to gradually establish a social medical insurance system in line with the socialist market economy.

There are so many shortcomings and problems in the current medical system that it requires a new social medical insurance system be established gradually in the future.

Along with the development of the economy and the deepening of the reform, the medical system established in the early 50s under the product economy has begun to show some shortcomings and problems that cannot be overlooked. Departments concerned and experts have reached the concerted understanding that the medical system reform must be pushed forward enthusiastically.

Medical system reform is an important component of social security system reform. China's current free and labor protection medical system was set up in the early 1950s on the basis of the supply system during the war by learning from the then Soviet Union. In the past forty years, the system has played an important role in keeping the vast number of workers in good health, promoting economic development and maintaining social stability and unity. The shortcomings and problems that showed up along with the economic development and deepening reform should not be ignored. The main problems are: (a) The medical expenses are all covered by the state and enterprises without a reasonable fund-raising mechanism. (b) Neither the provider nor the receiver of medical service is economically accounted for and there is no controlling mechanism. (c) Medical security has a narrow coverage without a scientific and rational management system. (d) There are huge wastes and insufficient medical care for some workers.

In the past few years, departments concerned in the Central Government, provinces and cities made many meaningful experiments in the reform. Different provinces and cities respectively carried out the reform to a different extent. To epitomize it, they have implemented the reform in the following four aspects:

(a) Universal implementation of linking the free medical care and labor protection medical expenses with individuals' proper partial payment; (b) about one million workers in eighty cities and counties in some provinces started the practice of pooling medical expenses for retired workers and those who suffer from serious illness; (c) some cities and counties in twenty-five provinces began to let hospitals manage medical expenses for their workers; (d) Hainan Province and Shenzhen City started the experiment in the reform in medical insurance system.

On the aim of the medical system reform. The aim and goal of China's medical system reform is to gradually establish a social medical insurance system that corresponds to the socialist market economy and productivity on the basis of current free medical care and labor protection. It includes the establishment of a medical insurance fund system with the fund jointly raised by the state, employers and individuals, the establishment of a proficient binding mechanism of medical expenses that guarantees the workers' basic medical needs and ends waste to the extent possible, and plan to establish a unified medical insurance institution and gradually promulgate and perfect regulations and decrees on social medical insurance.

On the raising of medical insurance fund. The fund is raised jointly by the state, employers and individuals. The amount raised by the state and employers remains as the current one without changing the current channels. Its ways may be changed from the current appropriation of medical expenditure to a collection of a certain percentage of the total wage along with the reform of the financial budget system. In 1991, the total wage of the state departments, institutions, state-run enterprises and large-size collective-run enterprises is 300 billion yuan, while medical expenses make up 9.1 percent of the total wage, roughly 30 billion yuan. The part that an individual pays may start with 1 percent of his or her wage, which will amount to an annual collection of 3.3 billion yuan. Along with economic development, increased workers' income and the advancement of medical technology, the medical insurance premium paid by the state, employers and individuals will be adjusted step by step.

On the management of the fund. The fund will be a large amount, which should be managed at different levels with each account. At the beginning, it may be divided into several funds such as a medical insurance fund for governmental departments and institutions and one for workers of urban enterprises. With a view to diversifying the coverage of risks for serious illness, the superior medical insurance institution may set aside a special fund for it. The special fund will be centrally managed and used as a whole. Along with structural reform, the state may set up social security administrative institutions, including those for medical insurance, which are to conduct macro-management. Corresponding institutions, which are mainly to take care of matters such as policy, rules and standards, may be set up in different localities. In the meantime, non-profit offices should be set up to be responsible for fund-raising, verification, management, registration and payment. They should be separated from enterprises.

On the payment from an individual worker. After the establishment of the social medical insurance system, a worker will pay twice annually. The first payment is 1 percent of his total wage. In 1991, the average annual wage income of workers in government departments, institutions, state-run enterprises and large-size collective-run enterprises is 2,430 yuan. One percent of it, 24 yuan, means a worker would pay 2 yuan a month on the average. On the score of low wage income it may be done on the basis of wage increase for workers or a certain subsidy provided. The second payment is the small amount of medical expenses that a worker pays at the beginning of his employment. At present, 80 to 90 percent of all the government departments and institutions and over 80 percent of the medium and small-size enterprises have adopted the method of linking free medical care and labor protection medical expenses with individuals' proper partial payment. Workers now basically accept it psychologically, so it should be continued. Nevertheless, there should be regulations on maximum payment, i.e., medical insurance institutions should be responsible for the part above five percent of the worker's annual wage income. The highest average annual medical expenses is 117 yuan for each worker according to national statistics. So, medical reform will embody the superiority of the socialist system and workers will accept it as well.

On the question of enlargement of medical insurance and coverage. As far as new and small collectives, private enterprises and the Chinese side in joint ventures are concerned, a total of 10 million workers in the whole country should enter into the social medical security plans. These people, 1.84 million workers in private enterprises, 3 million Chinese workers in joint ventures and 4 to 5 million workers in small enterprises should be included. Some 8 million self-employed businessmen and 240,000 to 150,000 owners of private enterprises in urban areas are encouraged to enter into the plans at their own expense. It is important to study and solve problems of medical insurance for the 900 million farmers. In the past few years, the collective economic power was weakened and the co-operative medical care in rural areas is basically dismembered. Eighty percent of them are in a state without medical security while feudal superstition popped up, quack medicine ran amuck and fake and low quality medicine flooded into the countryside. This caused resentment among the broad masses of farmers. Hence, the problem of medical security for farmers is strikingly placed in front of the government. Farmers need more assistance from the Party and government to solve their medical care problems.

About the policy on different categories of people. No change (to medical care) will be made for retired cadres whose service began before the founding of the People's Republic China. By the end of 1991, there were 1.93 million of them, and the number will not grow. They have made contributions to the founding of New

China. Their work units shall pay for them, and there will be no partial individual payments when they enter into medical insurance plans. Retired workers should be catered to for a certain extent as far as payment percentage is concerned. At present, there are 22 million retired workers throughout the nation with an annual increase of 6 percent, that is, 1.2 million each year. The retired workers with low income but complicated illness should be cared for. College students enjoy free medical care, but should take part in the reform. They are young and healthy. The main purpose for them to take part in the reform is to develop their conscience of payment, and it will help reduce wastes and losses.

The establishment of a social medical insurance system that corresponds to the socialist market economy is a gigantic systematic project that involves various sides, huge difficulties and sensitive policies. It cannot be achieved overnight. Before the establishment of a new system, measures that proved effective should be kept, so as to avoid a vacuum in the course of establishing a new system and prevent another big increase of medical spending. It is essential to push the new system gradually by gaining experience.

It is imperative to have a fundamental reform of the old health economic operational mechanism, and to establish a new one that corresponds to the socialist market economy.

The aim of medical insurance should be for health care, instead of medical care, because the latter has a much less significance. Only by keeping in good health, can productivity be liberated. Once productivity has developed and the economy goes up, the comprehensive national strength will be enhanced and the people's livelihood improved. The principle of medical insurance should serve production and the masses rather than being limited by monetary matters. Of course this does not mean neglecting economic issues. The goal of the reform should be for the establishment of a medical insurance system with Chinese characteristics, mainly in multi-channel fund-raising, multi-layer insurance plans, multi-function medical institutions and a socialized managing system.

According to experiences of Shanghai, Shenzhen, Hainan,

Beijing and Jilin, the key to the achievement of the goal lies in the fundamental reform of the old health economic operational mechanism and the establishment of a new one that corresponds to the socialist market economy.

Inconsistent operational mechanism will result in no guarantee for medical care and huge wastes. Where does the money for health care and medical care go? This is the key question for China's medical insurance plans. Importance should be attached to the correct handling of the relationship between reform and preventive health care, between reform and medicine manufacturing plants and between the reform and medicine supply and sales departments. In the meantime, the legal rights of workers in enterprises and staff of governmental departments should be protected to the letter in the course of the reform.

Some specialists put forward the question of choices of medical insurance plans. In fact, all reforms involve the question of choosing plans. In making the choice, the following two factors should be taken into consideration. One is what is the motivation under the plan, while the other is how big is the chance for choice under the plan. If these two questions are studied, an economically rational plan may be found. These two questions are particularly sensitive in regard to medical insurance plans. If free medical care is contracted to a hospital one day and may be contracted to enterprises the next day, the shifting back and forth does not solve the question: what's the people's motivation? People's basic action is an action for maximum interests. What will happen under these actions? These questions are not sufficiently studied, neither is the chance for choices sufficient. It is imperative to bring market mechanism into full play, so that people will have various plans to choose from.

(2) Establishment of a medical insurance model and framework that suits China's reality.

A medical security system with different contents, at various levels and in many forms should be established.

The Chinese government attaches great importance to the development of health care. China's health work has accomplished marked achievements with some major indexes above developing countries by properly utilizing health resources and emphasizing preventive and grassroots work, though China's average GNP per capita is still quite low. In past decades, China has reached a relatively high health care level with relatively low material investment. The developing trend seems that along with the enlargement of medical insurance coverage, its fund will become the main resources for the health care fund. Thus, the effective use of the fund by medical services will become an important subject for the study of medical insurance plans.

The primary goal of the reform should serve to improve medical service, promote the development of medical science and technology and enhance gradually the development of the national economy. Secondly, the bodies that provide funds for medical services, which are financial departments at various levels, all the enterprises and individuals, should continuously increase the percentage of investment, only to meet the needs of the reform. Thirdly, it is necessary to ensure the basic medical needs of the masses, as well as rational and effective use of health care resources. Fourthly, it is equally necessary to take into consideration the principle of the investors' intention for effective use of his money as well as the need of a sound development of the health care cause.

On the establishment of fund-raising mechanism that suits China's reality. China practices the principle that all fund-raising parties jointly take risks. At present, two groups of workers are involved in fund-raising. The first group consists of staff of governmental organizations and institutions and workers of state-run and collective enterprises. The government and enterprises take care of their medical expenses. Basically, it is a free medical care system. Facts have shown that along with the development of medical science and technology and continuous betterment of medical service and people's livelihood, their requirements for medical security continues to grow, faster than the improvement of living standards. So it won't meet the need by only relying on the limited resources of the government and enterprises. This is an arguing point for the theory that medical expenses have become a heavy burden for governments at various levels and enterprises. The second group consists of independent laborers, urban and rural residents, who constitute more eighty percent of the national population. They rely on themselves for medical expenses, instead of free medical care from the government, which only gives them support by pricing, in their favor, medical charges and charges in preventive health care. The government takes care of part of their expenses while they are responsible for the major part. The reality is that in a big country with a population of 1.2 billion, it is unrealistic for the government to provide for all the medical expenses, which must, instead, be jointly shared by the government, employers and individuals. Naturally, governments at various levels should increase their investment in health care security, fix scientific and reasonable quotas and percentages, and adjust them in time with the change of the situation so as to ensure normal investment and steady growth of medical insurance fund. It is equally necessary to work out different medical care plans in different forms to serve different people so that the medical needs of different groups of people are met, to expand the different forms of medical care plans that center on individuals' insurance. Now in rural areas, it is essential to expand current and effective co-operative medical care practices to solve the problem of medical expenses of the 800 million farmers with the mutual-aid method.

On the establishment of a special medical managing institution to manage and coordinate in a comprehensive way. The development of medical care needs the establishment of a social security committee to coordinate social security affairs. One of the leaders from the State Council shall be appointed as chairman of the committee because the medical security matter involves many departments and needs leadership from the government. Under the committee there will be a national medical insurance administration acting as the office for the committee to give guidance, coordination and supervision and oversee medical insurance affairs throughout the country. Governments above the county level shall have corresponding administrations of their own. Besides, it is necessary to establish and perfect medical insurance business offices, that is, set up separate medical insurance agencies whose job is to work out concrete plans, organize and coordinate implementation of the plans and raise, use and manage the fund in accordance with law.

On the establishment and perfection of the legal system for medical insurance. A sound legal system marks the civilization of a country. China's social security and medical insurance should be on the legalization track as soon as possible. At present there are some rules and regulations on free medical care and labor protection for enterprises, but there is no such rules on medical insurance for other groups of the population. In making laws and regulations on medical security or insurance, the duty, right and obligation of governments at various levels, medical insurance institutions, policy holders and the insurant shall be explicitly defined, so that all sides will have rules to follow.

Comprehensive coordination in the reforms. The medical system reform, a complicated and extensive project, needs the concern and support from various departments and from all walks of life. The reform in social medical security should go along with reforms in wage, accounting system, price, health administration, medicine manufacture and sales and social security. In one word, the reform and all other reforms are interrelated and interdependent. Moreover, the booking practice in the medical field should be straightened out and the state subsidy and charging practice should be reformed. Current Chinese medical services practice a budget to refund the balance, so they have to rely on fee charges as the resource for development and expansion. If hospitals want to develop along the direction of the market, they must reform the booking and accounting practice and ways of fee charges, so as to maintain self-development, adopt themselves to the socialist market economy and meet the need of social security. Medicine, including medicinal materials, is a special commodity to prevent and cure illness, so the reform of manufacturing, supply, sale and business principle of medicine particularly needs strengthening the control of pharmaceutical plants and the quantity and quality control. Fake medicine is a serious problem in China now because of loose management of medicine production. It is essential to produce expensive medicine of good quality as much as inexpensive ones of the same quality, to meet the need of different groups of people. At the same time, it is necessary to strengthen education in prevention. The medical care system reform is one of the most difficult in the social reforms at present. It involves people's economic capability as well as their psychological capability to adapt themselves to the reform. For a long time, China has practiced free medical care and workers have taken it for granted and their wages do not include that part so they find it psychologically hard to pay by themselves.

It is important to adhere to the strategic health policy of putting prevention in the first place. By sticking to the policy, China has achieved all-round success in health care and gained from its investment. According to experiences in China and other countries, China's medical insurance should also adhere to putting prevention in the first place. Only by doing so, can the lowest investment yield the highest output. Besides heightening people's understanding of preventive health care, it is necessary to spend more on preventive health care.

The goal of China's medical insurance is correct, but the method of fund separation is not free of worry. The structure of fund-raising might be a combination of state-run enterprises with private enterprises.

The most favorable point for China's medical insurance is that China has not set up a gigantic managing system like that of the United States. If China is led astray, it would be more difficult to turn back. Now the United States finds it particularly difficult to change it when politics is involved. From the angle of policies and management, China should make clear its current goal. Pertinent documents show that to develop medical insurance and keep people in good health is a central task and basic social duty. This is very important. The goal of the medical system of different countries is not always the same, and now China has its clear goal. The central and provincial governments have been aware of the two key questions, that is, the question of increase and that of medical insurance expenditure. Since the goal and questions are dealt with, next naturally comes how to reach the goal. Obviously, as far as staff and workers of enterprises are concerned, the new medical insurance plans will meet obstacles when they come into effect.

Two documents have mentioned a very important point, i.e., the clause on prevention need to play a forcible role in the medical insurance plan that has been put forward. The medical care plan pushed by the U.S. government is the biggest public medical care project of the U.S., involving 80 million people, but there is a tiny part on prevention, much of which is still being discussed. In China the aging problem itself is quite a big issue for system designing.

China has made clear the two goals that seem contradictory. One is that the medical insurance plan is for all and the other is to lower the cost of medical insurance. In fact, they do not contradict each other. The fact is that before the plan covers everybody, it is impossible to control medical insurance expenses. It finds a similar situation in the United States, where it is guaranteed that everyone buys an insurance policy to cut down expenses. Many countries in the world, including China, adopt the indirect fund-raising method to provide medical insurance to those who are not medically insured. As a result, it usually has to use this expensive and wasteful method to maintain the system. The American way is primarily to provide large subsidies to hospitals and spend a great deal of money on emergencies for those who need medical care. So the only way out is to expand the coverage of medical insurance to all, otherwise, the increase in costs will go beyond control.

Another similar problem is that according to the hard experience of the United States, it is essential to integrate risks with the whole population. One of the reasons is that in the United States, such a rich country, there are still thirty-five million people who do not have medical insurance. This is the reality of the private insurance business. There is a certain risk ratio for people of different ages or of different categories, and it usually turns out that those who need medical insurance most pay the highest premiums because their risk is the greatest. This is called reverse selection, that is, those who need help most are most willing to buy an insurance policy. So, if those who do not need insurance do not buy insurance policy, the expenses on medical insurance will be extremely high, and it will almost make medical insurance impossible.

Another idea is to separate the fund-raising for serious illness insurance from that for other illness insurance. The question of separation of fund-raising is disturbing. The first question is prevention. Which segment of the whole system should it go to? In fact, those who hope to have insurance against major diseases pay all their attention to prevention. Ninety percent of the quit-smoking publicity is done by health insurance companies, instead of government. The simple reason is that companies try to prevent people from falling seriously ill through publicity in order to reduce their expenditure. This is to say that the designing of the socialist market economic mechanism might have to take an overall consideration of insurance interests, or the combination of economic interests and the medical insurance interests. The above-mentioned smoking example is a case in point, so are fitness exercises and dieting. There will be problems if one is separated form the other. The second major problem is serious illness developed from minor illness. If a health hospital is to be established, we hope that doctors and medical staff will do their best to help us avoid developing serious illness. In other words, we do not want to establish a medical system that shifts the burden of expenses onto others. Unfortunately, China's traditional medical insurance was just like that. It is possible that China may establish a system wherein people get medical insurance when they fall ill. This does not mean we do it intentionally, but it is an existing problem in some countries.

In today's world, there are mainly three basic models as far as medical insurance structure is concerned. It is the combination of public-owned and private-owned as in the United States. The Netherlands has the only similar one as that of the United States. Sixty percent of Dutch insurance funds comes from private enterprises, while those who are not insured in private insurance companies automatically come under governmental insurance plans. This is different from that of the United States, and it may produce competition. In the United States, there is no competition between the public and private insurance business because the public one is for those who are unable to pay the premium of private insurance companies or are not accepted by them. While in the Netherlands, the government has made rules to encourage competition in providing insurance between the public-owned and private-owned insurance. The second model is based on the relationship of employers and employees. Take Germany as an example. Germany has an insurance system with strong participation by employers, and it has shown great success. Nevertheless, it started with a rapid increase of expenditure at the beginning. There is the problem of the employers' burdens in it. In the United States, employers are strongly opposed to it, and it went even as far as one employer is willing to pay employers of another trade, because the problem of expenditure may have impact on employers' competitiveness. Expenditure is not only a problem of premium but also expenses on system management and operation. This is what the employers are concerned about. The strong point of the model is that it does not need to set up a governmental administrative organization to operate it. If there is competition, there is a market with many participants. A German company with a staff of hundreds of thousands is more competitive than those individuals when they buy medical insurance policy at the market. Still another suggestion is that China establish a government-run insurance business, with two categories. One is the Canadian type: the government is the only organizer and contributor. According to its practice, one may arrive at the conclusion that it is quite good. But some people in the American administration do not think so. They feel there are many problems such as expensive medical care and voluntariness. The other is the Swedish type. Take the United Kingdom, for an example. Though the government does not employ staff in insurance, it is directly involved in the business operation. There are problems of long waiting periods, piled-up cases and increases of expenses. In short, the problem is whether the government should employ, manage or conduct daily routine. This is no longer raising funds for but providing insurance. Most people do not believe the British system is a success. A feasible choice for China is the combination of the public-owned and private-owned.

2. The Control of Medical Expenditure

(1) The current medical expenditure is so big, and increases so fast, that control of it must be strengthened.

China now faces a universal problem of rapid growth of medical expenses. In academic and policy discussions, there are two clear approaches to solving the problem. One is that individuals be responsible for a certain amount of their expenses in order to curb their actions and reduce waste. The other is to solve the problem caused by actions in the medical services. In past years, China has been enacting medical system reform, and hospitals have a more striking inclination to business. This has aroused criticism from the public media. This is an operational problem of increase of medical charges. Today, countries in the world are contemplating how to reasonably restrict actions by medical services at the same time as they revitalize them, such as giving subsidies to hospitals. The question of how to provide rational subsidies to medical services and restrict their irrational actions so that the whole society's medical expenditure is under control deserves further exploration.

One of the problems of the current medical system is the lack of a binding mechanism of medical expenditure.

Some specialists pointed out that one of the problems of current medical care reform is the lack of a binding mechanism. Neither the provider nor the recipient of medical service holds economic responsibility, which goes to the third party, the state and enterprises. Under this situation, there is a large quantity of waste and loss. Long sick leave for minor illness, pretentious sick leaves and taking advantage of one man's free medical care for the whole family are quite common. The total expenses of the free medical care and labor protection medical care in 1978 was 2.7 billion yuan while that for 1991 reached 30 billion yuan. The past few years saw faster increases of medical expenditure, over 10 percent for both 1988 and 1989, and it fell back to 14 percent in 1991 but exceeded the 11.7 percent for the year's financial budget. The first half of last year began to witness a rising tendency with an increase of more than 20 percent.

There are some reasonable factors in the big increase. First, more and more people are entitled to free medical care. There was an annual increase of three million people in past years, that is to say, each year, three million people were employed by government organizations, institutions, state-run or collective-run enterprises. Second, there are more and more cases of aging diseases. There are wastes and losses due to the lack of a binding mechanism and strict management. It is learned that it is common in the Northeast 1 million yuan of medical expenses for state-run enterprises of 3,000 workers, or about two million yuan for those of 4,000 to 5,000 workers are on credit.

There should be a dual binding force, both on the patients and hospitals. In past years, various places conducted exploration of reform. The primary binding force on individuals is to let the individual pay a proper portion of the free medical care and labor protection medical expenses. In past years, the low percentage of partial payment by the individuals did not yield a marked result in cutting down medical expenses. On the other hand, there should be a binding force on hospitals, which receive approximately four billion yuan of subsidies each year from the state financial department to balance their budgets. The actual annual expenditure of all the hospitals needed some forty billion yuan, or 38.5 billion yuan to be exact. Hospitals had to make earnings of their own to make up for the difference between state subsidies and their actual spending. It was understandable that hospitals, under the system, developed ways to increase their earning. They targeted those who were entitled to free medical care. As a matter of fact, it turned out to be a financial transfer, that is, part of the expenses on the free medical care and labor protection medical care turned into hospitals' earnings. The major practice now is that cities in 25 provinces and municipalities directly under the Central Government are experiencing free medical expenses contracted to hospitals. Under this plan, hospitals may use the surplus of the contracted sum for their own while the hospitals, enterprises and financial departments will be jointly responsible for the part exceeding the contracted figure. This has contained the sharp rise of medical expenses to a certain extent.

There are many causes for the increase in medical expenses, but the key lies in the strengthening of macroadjustment, to control the increase of medical expenses within the economic growth rate.

The 1980s, especially the late 1980s, saw a rapid increase of medical expenses in China, which drew concern from the whole society. From 1980 to 1992, the average annual increase of medical expenses for workers of state-run enterprises was 16.3 percent and that from 1986 to 1990 was 20.4 percent, while the average annual GNP growth for the corresponding periods was 14.8 percent and 15.6 percent. The increase of medical expenses was faster than that of the GNP, among which the free medical care expenses saw an average annual increase of 20.8 percent for the period between 1980 and 1992 and 24.5 percent from 1986 to 1990. The increase of financial expenditure for the corresponding periods was respectively 11 percent and 13.4 percent. The increase rate of free medical care expenses is faster than that of financial expenditure. There are many causes. Concrete analysis arrives at the following:

(a) The increase of people entitled to medical security benefits. In 1980 there were 78.19 million workers in state-run enterprises and governmental organizations and 87.81 million in 1985, an increase of 9.62 million, with an average annual increase of 1.92 million. It reached 100,030,040 in 1992, an increase of 15.65 million over that in 1985, with an average annual increase of 3.5 million. This caused the increase in medical expenses.

(b) The aging of the population and workers and the changes of disease patterns. China's life expectancy has reached seventy years from thirty-five in the year before liberation in 1949. In 1990, the population of those above sixty years old was 92.22 million, 8.6 percent of the whole population as compared with 7.8 percent in 1982. Retired workers amounted to twenty million in

1990, 16.3 percent of all those employed in the state-run businesses and governmental organizations. Along with the aging of the population, rapid development of the national economy, advancement of science and technology, development of health care and the strengthening of social preventive work, the traditional biomedicine patterns are gradually changing. Infectious diseases fell back from the first killer before the founding of the People's Republic of China to the 9th while chronic diseases like cancer, cerebrovascular disease and heart disease gradually became the top three. Statistics of 1991 showed that in some cities cancer became the number one killer, cerebrovascular disease the second and heart disease the third and 58.3 percent of the total morality was caused by the top three killers. These diseases are hard to cure and cost more money. According to surveys in Shanghai, the hospitalization charges of those above sixty-five years old is 1.6 times over that of those under sixty-five years old.

(c) The increase of the cost of medicine and medicinal materials, as well as changes and improvement of medicine. According to statistics, the price index of medicine in 1980 was 100 while that in 1989 rose to 185.3. If that in 1985 was 100 and the one in 1989 was 165.4. In recent years, medicine improved very fast, for instance, drug stores in a city had several hundred new medicines in 1987, with a quantity of 3.6 times over that in 1980. This led to rising of medical costs.

(d) Cost increase of medical equipment thanks to technological progress. Along with the economic development and opening to the outside world in past years, some big precision instruments and equipment, such as CT, JCT and magnetic resonant image accelerator have increased prices. Such equipment and instruments are very expensive. One magnetic resonant image examination costs more than 1,000 yuan, while one CT examination costs 300 to 400 yuan. The fast progress of diagnostic technique helps diagnosis as much as increases medical expenses.

(e) Mal-management. Some hospitals tended to gain for economic income, so some doctors gave prescription for fast earnings or used unnecessary diagnostic examination methods for higher charges. Some pharmaceutical plants sold low quality medicine, or fancy packed medicine for higher profits. There were both objective and subjective causes for the increase of medical expenses. According to surveys in Shanghai, the price increase of medicine from 1980 to 1990 made the medical expenses increase by fifty percent. The advancement of medical equipment caused an additional increase.

The following measures may be adopted to strengthen the control of medical expenditure.

(a) To strengthen macro-adjustment. An important factor for the fast increase of medical expenditure is the lack of adjustment at the national level. It is inevitable that medical expenses will continue to increase gradually in the future, because along with the economic development and the improvement of people's livelihood, people's medical needs, the development of medical technology and the advancement of medical equipment will certainly have an important impact on medical expenditure. It is necessary to keep the increase of medical expenditure within a reasonable rate, namely, to control the increase within an appropriate pace with the nation's economic development. What is appropriate and proper, and how to measure it, deserve study. According to international experience, it primarily means that the rate of increase of medical expenditure should correspond to the growth rate of GNP, as in Canada and the United Kingdom. The two increase rates should be balanced and correspond to each other. When the increase rate exceeds that of GNP, ways should be worked out to reduce medical expenses. If the rate is under that of the GNP, it is necessary to increase expenses properly. It is highly necessary for us to maintain the increase rate of medical spending at the pace of the increase of the GNP.

(b) To guarantee basic medical care and control of non-basic and extra medical care. Free medical care and labor protection medical care are subject to medical insurance. According to the principle of social security, it is only to meet the basic medical need of workers, who should try other approaches, such as buying insurance policies of commercial insurance companies to cover their non-basic and higher medical needs. Anyway, it is a new issue that needs a clear definition of basic and non-basic medical care. Departments concerned are advised to study and work out a "definition" as soon as possible. An initial idea is that some non-basic medical care, such as nutrition, fitness recuperation, plastic surgery, beautification, dieting, or high standard hospitalization are listed as non-basic and spending on them should not be reimbursed.

(c) To share medical spending. Turn free medical care into one that is shared by the state, enterprises and individuals. This is an effective method of controlling irrational increase of medical expenditure. There are two steps: one is that enterprises as well as individuals pay the premium, the other is that a worker will pay a small amount of the medical charges when he or she falls ill. Its primary purpose is to control over-spending for medical care. As for the rate, it may be low at the beginning, because China has a low wage system. The rate may be increased along with the raise of workers' wages. The principle is to ensure that workers can stand it and wastes are controlled.

(d) To control the consumption of medicine. The consumption of medicine takes up more than fifty percent of the medical expenditure, so the control of medicine consumption is the key. Two approaches may be under consideration. One is the control of manufacturing and sale of medicine. Medicine is a special commodity, the production of which should be under control even in market economy. Hence, the manufacturing, supply and sale system should undergo appropriate reform. The combination of planned adjustment and market adjustment should be used in managing the production of therapeutic medicine. Medicine for basic medical care will be manufactured in a planned way, supplied as it is needed and its price strictly controlled. The other is the strict control of imported medicine. A medicine list for reimbursement under medical insurance plans should be worked out. The current practice is that there is a list the medicine on which cannot be reimbursed. It should be changed to a list for reimbursement, to effectively control the consumption of medicine and restrict unreasonable consumption.

(e) To import big precision equipment in a planned way to overcome blind importation. Statistics showed that a total of

1,000 CTs were imported, about 600 through normal channels and 400 through abnormal channels. It is not too many to have, one CT for one million people, but the distribution is very irrational, mostly concentrated in Tianjin, Beijing, Shanghai and coastal provinces like Liaoning, Jiangsu and Zhejiang. It is necessary to strengthen macro-management to have a rational layout of the equipment. It is important to emphasize import and to appraise the imports, particularly the end-results.

(f) To contract medical care to hospitals and have patients treated in grassroots hospitals whenever possible, so as to cut down medical expenses. In the future, medical insurance institutions may fix several hospitals as their contracted hospitals to provide convenient medical care to workers, intensify competition and better service. Hospitals and medical insurance institutions should, on a voluntary basis, choose each other to sign a contract, which includes requirements of coverage, items and quality, fee standard, contracted period, etc. It is important to work out regulations on verification of contracted hospitals and on treating out-patients, and to further perfect and adjust regulations on medical charges. It is necessary to intensify preventive medical care and health education.

(g) To perfect responsibility management. It is imperative to strengthen education in professional morals, and work out regulations to curb unscrupulous and unprincipled prescription, unchecked examinations and illegal charges, to control precision equipment examination in particular.

(h) To strengthen prevention.

It is necessary to control inappropriate expenses on the one hand, and to reform unreasonable expenditure patterns in hospitals and raise hospital charges, help develop health care causes on the other.

Medical expenses are on the rise in a special way. Everybody believes that should be controlled. In fact, it is one side of the coin and everyone should see the other side. Medical expenses in China are at a very low level with unbalanced layout, the annual average per capita is fifty-six yuan, less than ten U.S. dollars. Even with this figure, there is a sharp difference between rural and urban areas. It is higher in medium-size and large cities while much lower in rural areas. So it poses not a question of how to control but how to develop rural medical care institutions and provide due medical services. It is an extraordinarily heavy task for China.

There are 2.5 billion out-patients each year in China, and the average expense for one out-patient is 13.7 yuan.

At present, medical institutions are developing rapidly, especially in coastal areas, and some hospitals may be compared to those in developed countries in their size but not in facilities, while hospitals at the county level cannot meet the basic medical need of farmers. China faces an important issue of investing more in medical care for bigger development.

There is a gigantic gap between the wages of medical workers in China and that in developed countries. In China, wages of medical workers are not high. There might have been some increase in the past year or so for certain sectors. But in general, the average wage is lower than the medium of the whole nation.

In analyzing China's medical expenses, an understanding shall be reached in the following two aspects. There is a heavy workload to intensify control on the one hand, and there is the need to attach importance to the development of health care and increase of medical charges on the other hand. China, a big country with a population of 1.2 billion, has to consider the two aspects.

It is of paramount importance to control expenses and stop irrational phenomena. The crux of the problem lies in the following aspects. First, almost all of the medical expenses for workers in state-run and state-owned enterprises are covered. This stimulates personal consumption because individuals do not pay but take it as their personal right, so they try everything to enjoy it as if they are losing if they fail to enjoy the right. When workers take medicine home, not only they but the whole family will take it because many people understand the function of general medicine for common illness. This has stipulated the increase of individuals consumption.

Moreover, mal-management of hospitals has existed for a

long time. Hospitals have stayed where they stood, to say nothing of development. They even could not keep simple production, because hospitals have been keeping budgets to refund the balance. Nevertheless, there is something in it, for government might reduce its direct financial expenditure. Therefore, the government allowed hospitals to increase medicine prices by fifteen percent, to distribute at retail price. This provides hospitals with chances to increase their income on medicine.

Second, the structure of hospital expenditure is irrational. The value of doctors' work is not, at least not very well, embodied in hospital management. In the past, the clinic registration charge was only 5 fen, later increased to 20 or 30, or 50 fen in some big cities. Now the admission charge for ordinary parks is up to 1 or 2 yuan. One has to pay 1 yuan to buy an admission ticket to see monkeys in the zoo, while he has only to pay 20 fen to see the doctor. Doctors' value to diagnose is not manifested. Hospitalization charges are also very low. When one has to put up for one night in a hostel or a hotel, he has to pay dozens of yuan, even several hundred yuan, while a patient only pays seven yuan per night on the average for hospitalization. These distorted charges caused great difficulties in the development of hospitals. The proper channel of increase to meet the demand of hospital development is smooth, while hospitals have to rely on medicine and new equipment to make more money. Otherwise, they could hardly develop. Of the financial expenditure in the medical expenses of the whole country, governmental medical expenditure makes up about nineteen percent. This cannot meet the need of hospital development but stimulates unprincipled and unscrupulous prescriptions. If this situation is to be changed, it is necessary to clarify what a hospital is. Now it is called a tertiary industry, while it was called a public welfare institution in the past. Is it a public welfare or an institution? No matter what it is, it has to adopt business-like procedure in face of the current trend toward a socialist market economy. Since it is to develop business-like services, it must establish the principle of cost and profits, which will not only meet the current need of hospitals but also their development. But, at present, the government still has a quite tight control on prices concerning medical care, which is the last control by the Price Bureau. Prices in other fields have broken the control system. We call on hospitals to break away from the price system under the state control.

The above-mentioned points are analysis, instead of shifting some of the hospital's responsibilities, with an intention to help hospitals move onto normal business track, so that its value of service will be respected and thereupon, measures will be taken to check abnormal and illegal practices. As for hospitals, the control of expenditure has two connotations. First, to put hospitals onto the normal business track and stop mal-practices. Second, to adopt a double approach to curb excessive spending by individuals. Individuals have to buy insurance policy first and then take more responsibilities for their expenses. The 5 to 10 percent of all the medical expenses that an individual was responsible for in past years seemed too small a percentage to control individuals' irrational consumption. It should be increased by 10 to 20 percent, and it should be followed by a corresponding increase of pay. The resolution of the problem will certainly have a positive impact on the control of individual consumption. It is necessary to strengthen management of hospitals and illegal and unscrupulous prescriptions should be dealt with and examined by experts in a given period of time. In the past, insurance companies regularly examined every prescription to see if it was in line with regulations. But, in face of such a vast group of people, how many people will be involved to finish the examination of every prescription and diagnosis? It will be a figure beyond our ability. So the only practical way is to have regular random examinations to discipline and penalize unscrupulous practices by deducting budgets and reducing some insurance funds, with the aim of supervising hospitals' practices, strengthening their management and discipline and cutting down irrational charges from the patients. The few illegal practices will be punished according to law. Nevertheless, they are not the main causes of the increase of medical expenses. Of course, it is of paramount importance to intensify legislative work.

(2) The practice of medical insurance for everybody will lead to over-spending for medical care.

Some Chinese and foreign specialists aired different views on universal medical insurance for everybody, believing that people psychologically feel they are losing something if they do not go to see the doctor, thus it will lead to over-spending for medical care.

It is the inevitable road for state-owned institutions to follow the principle of joint responsibility shared by the three parties. As for the part by individuals, some suggested that individuals should contribute a certain amount to the medical insurance fund and pay part of the medical expenses. It is a good idea that individuals pay part of the expenses, but there seems no definite answer to individual's contribution to the insurance fund. The question lies in whether our health policy should encourage everybody to put prevention in the first place, and whether it will foster the mentality that one feels he or she is losing money because of previous contributions to the fund, so he goes to see the doctor even if he is not sick.

Moreover, a large number of workers, particularly young workers, seldom go to hospitals while only the minority fall ill. Hence, it is different from the old-age pension, in which case everybody's pension will be eventually honored. How about medical insurance? It is hard to say that one will not fall sick for his whole life, but compared with old-age pension, it is not cashed back in every case. So, the notion that everybody should contribute to medical insurance fund deserves assiduous study.

Apart from the binding mechanism on individuals, there has to be a binding mechanism on hospitals and enterprises. As for how to cut down hospital expenditure, it needs further study. In the case of enterprises, there is the question of whether the pool plan for serious illness will lead to the understanding that enterprises have less responsibilities because insurance institutions play a greater role.

As for collective-owned enterprises in cities and towns, joint ventures and private enterprises that have labor protection medical care without free medical care, they should establish a medical insurance system in line with the market mechanism. In rural areas, the establishment of a medical insurance fund may be under study. The resources are simple, with only the state appropriation, but there have been great changes in educational fund raised through many channels in past years. Rural hospitals should give a careful thought to it.

It is necessary to differentiate traditional medical insurance (accidental insurance) from the current insurance, which compensates for medical care. This will lead to medical over-spending due to personal psychological inclination. The structure of medical insurance should be given serious consideration.

The concept of insurance appeared in a conventional way in China about three thousand years ago. Later, a Royce Coffee Shop in London became well-known in the West and modern insurance developed therefrom. Traditional insurance refers to coverage of uncontrollable and unpredictable risks. When one is insured for calamity that he does not want to occur, he hopes that he does not have to seek compensation. Now we are far away from this kind of insurance but coming into health care. The causes of the big change are as follows:

First, we all need medical care. To a certain extent, one will need medical treatment during his life time and always need preventive medical care. Therefore, no doubt, we will all go for medical treatment now or later, and this is not something unpredictable.

Second, one may go to hospital if he is overweigt, or smokes, or something unexpected happens to him while he is doing something else. In another word, if I am insured, I probably will make others compensate me for what I have done. Another side of the issue is that those who regularly buy insurance policies tend to be those who consume the least of the insurance compensation. If we make a survey of metropolitans in the world, let's say almost all the countries in the world, we will find that the more complicated the structure of the population, the more one spends on medical insurance. This is not because they need more medical care but because they know how to determine their need and how to get the most expensive medical care.

When we talk about medical care, we all fall into a trap: in fact, in most countries there is no medical insurance, and what there is is prepaid medical expenses, or prepaid compensation. What is different from the compensation is the retirement pension that one has prepaid. It will happen only once, and he knows that it will certainly happen. But for medical insurance, one may never have to seek compensation while another may have to do it fifteen times in a week. All in all, the possibility of various situations is very big in regard of medical insurance. All this should give us food for thought to seriously consider all the encouragement and discouragement in establishing medical insurance. We all know that only part of those who buy medical insurance policies buy an accidental medical insurance policy. In the United States, it is less than eight percent each year. This refers to the insurance that the beneficiary family gets U.S. $30 million and 90 percent of the people do not need this kind of accidental insurance. In this sense, accident insurance is like elementary insurance. One begins to realize that this is the genuine accidental insurance for the unpredictable happening when he views the original sense of insurance. People will not rely on intentional gains from insurance compensation for accidental injury. The reason we mention this is there are such traps in many countries. To some extent, it is because people have not contemplated the difference between compensation and medical care and that between insurance and insurance in the original sense. If China can establish a prevention system against accidental calamity to some extent and the fund needed will be raised according to the situation in different localities, and the accidental calamity will bring tremendous economic threat and extremely serious problems to families, and if there is insurance against it, there will not be worries of participation and over-spending of the premium and people will not over-use the premium against the accidental calamity. In any country, spending on medical care is not an insured sum of money against accidental disaster. The Chinese people like to save money, want to protect it and use a method that enables them not have to prepay a premium that is less than their savings. If they do not have to spend money on the non-accidental insurance, they will be able to save the money.

It is suggested to establish "workers' health co-operatives." Some places may continue their insurance plan against accidental calamity, with prepaid premiums by the insured as they did in the past. At least workers should be allowed to form voluntary co-operatives. This is their mutual-aid insurance company. If they have to contribute to the company, their contributions may be the same as the prepayment that they will prepay the government. But they will do two or three things. First, they will do publicity work about health because as a result of their work the insured will get a refund from the money for medical care that has been saved. This may help develop a system with workers as the main body to push forward health work, to achieve striking economic results. Second, they can draw some funds. The actual expenses of the premiums against calamity by most people are relatively small in a given year.

Chapter V
Administration of China's Social Security System

1. The Administrative and Operational Mechanisms

(1) **The current administration of the social security system, which is departmentalized, disconnected, incoordinate and derelict, urgently needs the establishment of a unified administrative system.**

There are three alternative plans for the resolution of the problem.

Due to various historical reasons, the administration and operation of China's social security is divided. To solve the problem, departments concerned have made great efforts, but have not made much progress. Departmentalized, disconnected and derelict actions in handling daily routine severely impede the development and reform of the social security system. The key to speeding up the current reform, and pushing forward development, lies in the determination to straighten out the management.

Here are three alternative plans: The first alternative is to set up a Social Security Ministry under the State Council (social security bureau in provinces) to oversee the administrative work, and at the same time set up non-profit operational institutions responsible for the enforcement of laws on social security, the collection and payment of premium, the use and investment of the fund, etc. The second alternative is to establish a Social Security Commission under the State Council, consisting of leading members from the ministries of labor, health, personnel, civil affairs, finance, the bank, the State Planning Commission, the State Commission for Economic Restructuring, the All-China

Federation of Trade Unions, the industry and commerce administration and the insurance company. Its main job is to organize the study and work-out reform plans, and to coordinate the work among departments. The day-to-day work still remains as it is under various departments. The third alternative is to keep the current structure and continue the separation of management by labor, health, personnel and civil affairs departments with their insurance agencies doing the business on the basis of further clarification of their functions and job descriptions.

Each of the three plans makes sense. But on the whole, the first plan draws more attention. Some provinces, such as Hainan, Jilin and Guangdong, have either started experiments in unified leadership and management, or decided to set up separate social security companies, or to set up a labor insurance company and life insurance limited company.

The managing structure of social security reflects the particular political, economic and social content of a country. China should establish a unified managing organization.

The management structure reflects, to a great extend, a particular political, economic and social content. Then, how to select one from the many structures? Social security may be managed by a specialized governmental department. In some countries, along with the gradual development of social security system toward nearly full coverage of the whole population, an independent comprehensive managing organization is gradually forming. In other countries, a governmental management department is in charge of social security plans. Nevertheless, all governments, almost without exception, have always focused their attention on social security policy. In some countries, special agencies have been set up to take care of the matter. They have their own authority, to different extents, and the government sometimes has only indirect control of it, or just in name. These agencies are usually under the control of the board of directors, who respectively represent the employers, employees or the government. In some other countries, social security is under the control of an institution to a great extent, and often different ministries or managing institutions take care of different matters.

For instance, health and welfare departments may be responsible for pension and medical care projects, while labor departments are more inclined to employment affairs. In practice, this structure tends to be influenced by many factors, or some unreasonable factors. Politics, individuals or important factors of structural reform may have major impact. It is important to gradually link social security plans with government programs in other fields. China particularly has to go in for reforms in taxation, education, medical care and housing. But, most important of all is the question of unemployment relief, which needs close combination with employment service programs, and it is all the more true with the management at lower levels. In some countries, the unemployed person is required to register at the employment office. But the premium will be paid by other offices of social security. In other countries, the two are done in one office.

It is important to establish a social security committee for unified management.

Social security managing system should, with a unified administration and legislation, be under a special agency organized and led by the government. Now that the economic reform upholds separation of power and delegation of authority, then, why should it be under a unified management? The goal of China's reform is to establish a socialist market economy. There are at least two important aspects in the economy. On the one hand, its main body, enterprises, is an independent producer and responsible for its own profits and losses. On the other hand, there must be a nationwide market. Without a unified market, enterprises will have no place to perform. A unified market needs unified management and market regulations. Therefore, the two aspects are inter-dependent. Unified market means to get rid of obstacles, any obstacles that impede the circulation of commodities and goods, no matter whether they come from departments or local governments. One of the purposes is to liberate or free enterprises from social burdens so that they are able to enter the market for a fair competition on an equal footing. In a market economy, there should be free circulation of production factors, including funds, capital and labor. Without the circulation of labor, there will be no market economy. Labor forces, just like capital, compete with one another. Labor forces may flow freely between different enterprises, departments and places. Enterprises may choose workers as well as workers may choose enterprises. Only under free circulation, can all kinds of resources, including human resources, be best placed and most properly used for high micro- and macro-efficiency. If, within the scope of social security, there is no unified and consistent regulations, different departments and places will do their own thing, and it will create many visible and invisible obstacles, which are not in favor of the circulation of labor, the establishment of a unified market and the development of market economy. If so, it runs counter to the goal of a socialist market economy. Hence, it is necessary for a socialist market economy to establish a unified social security organization.

The actual situation is that due to the needs of reform and economic development, various departments and local governments developed faster than at the Central Government level in the construction and facility of social security. The Central Government was relatively slow in issuing new measures for nationwide reform, while some local governments tried many experiments and made great achievements. Some central departments, such as the Labor Ministry and Civil Affairs Ministry, also made experiments with good results, which are of great value. But eventually there will be a unified national social security system. It is a specific question then as of which department is in charge of it. It is necessary to establish a central organization in charge of the matter, whether it is the ministry of social security or social security commission. The latter may be better, because it involves many fields and departments, such as finance, health, labor, etc. It is difficult for any ministry to supervise, so it is better for a special organization, which is above ministries but under the State Council, to be in the position to coordinate and work out unified social security plans.

It is imperative to set up a unified organization to supervise social security for semi-vertical management.

With separated management by different ministries, provinces do not know which to follow, just like five dragons trying to harness the river while each one is doing his own thing. Any ministry may issue documents, and anybody may be in charge. Things will go along well if there is no contradiction. When there are contradictions without coordination, they have to go to the governor or the mayor for guidance. All walks of life vehemently request the establishment of a unified management system and a harmonious external environment. How to set up one? Some feel that the present conditions are not ready yet. A unified management needs the establishment of a commission based on the current ministries with a vice premier or state councilor at its head to coordinate policies. This is a small step forward and still of the format like several dragons harnessing the river. Some others have suggested that those in different ministries who are now handling social security work may be pooled together to form a social security ministry. Those who at the grassroots stress pragmatism as some others, standing high with a far and macro sight, hold that without the establishment of a social security system, economic development will meet obstacles. How about a small step forward by both taking into consideration a unified management and the reality? Thus, someone has proposed to establish the Ministry of Social Security.

There is a question of vertical supervision or local supervision whatever the organization is named. Now central departments do not have the power to appoint officials but only give policy guidance, which the local officials may follow if in their favor and may shut their ears to it if otherwise. There is no way to check and supervise. That is why it is imperative to have a vertical supervision system, just like the banks or taxation offices. Anyway, it may not be workable, if it is entirely separated from local government. As a result, a semi-vertical managing system is the answer. A draft regulation on old-age pension submitted to the State Council last November stated, it is important to intensify social security work, and the change of leading members of social security organization should have the approval of the superior organization. This means that local governments have the power to appoint, but have to notify the central departments before appointments. There is a binding force on both the local and the central authorities. Step by step, things will proceed smoothly and in a standardized fashion.

There is a staff problem. China now has a staff of 30,000 working on social security, and France has a staff of 180,000. France's population is only 5 percent of that of China. According to that ratio, China should have a staff of 3.6 million. China's management level is relatively low with less projects. Nevertheless, one million is needed in whatever case.

(2) The operational mechanism should follow the policy of the separation of administration, institution and enterprises.

At present, there are more discussions of which department should be in charge of social security work, but fewer studies of what and how the government might manage the matter. Now the government is running a lot of things which are not easy, neither of its realm, nor should it handle. Foreign experts think that there are twelve categories of management functions. According to Chinese way of classification, there are three parts. The first part is under the government; the second part is under institutions and offices; and the third part is under enterprises. This is the separation of government, institutions and enterprises.

Social security management should be considered according to its functions, and may be divided into policy-making, business-running and investment and operation.

Specialists felt the management was a quite complicated question and a thorny subject to discuss. Foreign specialists suggest that it is essential to contemplate its function according to which the management of social security is considered. The idea to clarify its functions and then manage is a quite good and scientific one. The function might not be entirely clear in China and needs further study and exploration. Social security may be roughly divided into three parts. First, the government works out general policies. Second, the management office or institutions implement policies. There is much work to do and it leaves much to be desired. Take old-age pensions, for an example. Enterprises are responsible for the great bulk of it. This cannot go on and enterprises should no longer hold the responsibility. The management must be socialized. This part should be in charge of collecting fees, reviewing qualification of entitlement to social security benefits and caring for the aged. Third, the application, operation and investment of the fund for the best end-result. This part should be separate. Again take old-age pension, for example. It does not refer to the pay-as-you-go money, but the accumulation, which is prepared for the peak period of old age. It involves a question of reserving and increasing the value, instead of simply depositing it in banks. It needs a fund management committee made up of representatives from various sides to supervise the funds investment. The investment of the fund should be different from the state financial budget or basic construction by the planning department, and it needs detailed booking. There should be a special institution in charge of the heavy workload, which should be combined with the economic construction and industrial policy. At the same time, old-age insurance may be divided into three parts, the legal basic insurance that is managed by non-business institutions, supplementary insurance by enterprises and individuals' savings. Enterprises' insurance and individuals' savings should adhere to voluntary principles and may go under the service coverage of insurance companies, which have explicit rules and regulations according to which the increased value of the fund should go to the account of the old-age insurance, rather than to insurance company itself.

The administration of social security should be separated from fund operation, which is done by "financial intermediary."

Some experts believe fund operation should be separated from administration, which is under the government to take care of policy, regulation, standards and daily routine, while the fund should handle the operation and increase of the fund value. The fund is not an administration but an organization formed under the economic principles, or "financial intermediary" as it is called in foreign countries. Its main purpose is to ensure the increase of fund value by good investments, which are called "institutional investment" abroad. These institutional investors should be more closely linked with state industrial policy, and under the guidance of which, they put large sums of investments in projects that ordinary enterprises are unwilling to invest in, or in basic industry and infrastructure that the country needs most. Besides administrative offices, intermediaries should be fully developed. This is not only conducive to the establishment of social security system, but also to the development of financial markets. The development of finance, financial intermediary system and financial market is inseparable from the perfection of the social security system.

Why is it particularly considered from the financial angle? The huge social security fund helps develop financial intermediary and develop institutional investors. In Western countries, the more developed the market economy, the faster the financial system develops. With the greater development of financial intermediaries, they will play a greater role as investors in the social economy. If the market economy develops and so do financial intermediaries, social security funds and medical funds, the intermediaries will gradually invest more than direct investment of the state. To develop financial intermediaries and bring into play institutional investors bear a great significance in the reform of the state ownership and greater significance than social security.

It is appropriate to have a unified operation and indirect investment.

It must be a non-profit organization appointed by the government to conduct unified, rather than scattered, operations. Take the old-age pension as an example. It will not do if an organization under the labor department takes care of old-age pension for workers in enterprises, one under the personnel department takes care of that for governmental staff, and one under the industry and commerce department takes care of that for private businessmen. This is neither in line with the principle of socialized management, nor in favor of the circulation of labor, the reduction of costs and saving of funds. It is socialized management in words but departmentalized when it comes to specific problems. It is hoped that the central authorities will make the determination as soon as possible. If not soon enough, the localities will have to establish unified operational setups first, because there should not be too many operational setups. Some departments under the State Council may think this is a foul play, but the local authorities have to do so.

The operational setups can only collect and distribute the fund, while financial institutions will mainly do the indirect investment, and it may call for tenders in the future. The fund will be given to those who guarantee the increase of value in a secure and effective way. The decision-making of investment direction should be considered in connection with the fund financial system. Take the old-age insurance fund, as an example. When the fund is insufficient, the central authorities shall make the decision if it is responsible, and the local authorities shall make the decision if it is responsible. The current practice is that the local authorities are in charge of the pool fund-raising, so if the fund is insufficient, the local authorities are responsible for either increasing the percentage or levy taxes on workers and of course the local authorities will make the policy decision on investment.

China should attach importance to democratic management and financial autonomy in social security.

China should attach importance to how to intensify democratic management. In the past, Chinese folks took the government as their "parents" and it was most secure to give their money to parents. But now the folks feel that it is insecure to let government take care of the money because the government has too much power. Just a word by the mayor, all the money will be used and all the departments find it hard to deal with. Therefore, the economic sector should be the first to learn and implement democratic management. Money-managing institutions should be autonomous, because the money should be taken as the private property of the insured, who have the right to form their own board of directors.

International specialists believe one problem for China's social security management is that enterprises are not aware of how to transit to the ways of social security after they become independent from the protection of the state. It includes retirement pension insurance, unemployment insurance, health insurance as well as the reduction of interests. And every social security branch, like those of retirement pension, industrial insurance, health insurance and unemployment insurance should have autonomy to a certain extent. In some countries, there is only one unified way of payment, so such branches do not have the problem of financial autonomy. The first question is whether the financial autonomy of these branches means a kind of priority or just an institution, namely, a social security institution supervising all the branches. In some countries, the privilege is left over from history, because it worked efficiently. China does not have that history. Apart from some exceptions, China, marching toward the world market, will overcome difficulties to protect the insured people and those who prepay the premium. It will form an exclusive setup for the security of clients, because different setups have different connections in social security. That is why there are heated debates over the idea of one institution to supervise all branches. Unemployment insurance has its particular problem: whether unemployment insurance should be managed in connection with employment service, or depart from the old social security system. Another approach is to separate the management of unemployment insurance from that of employment service and be put under social security. Anyway, it is a partly technical and partly political consideration. If this approach is adopted, there is no need for an unemployment office or employment service to manage unemployment insurance and it has at least one important point, that is, the collection of premium will be under concentrated management just like retirement pension and other premiums. At least, there will be some ordinary services. The second question is that the financial autonomy with governmental financial assistance means social security autonomy independent of government. This is chiefly a political choice and the independent authority of financial management is the guarantee of social security autonomy. There has always been debates on management autonomy in order not to mix up social security with government budgets and not to let government spend social security funds on other matters. In this situation, the government should formulate policies, regulations and decrees for autonomous institutions to follow. The third question is somewhat related to autonomy, that is, many people hold that the security fund should belong to the laborers. Legally speaking, it is not quite accurate, but it implies that in many countries, social security managing institutions are included in some committees and executive institutions. It may be based on three parties, namely, the employers or representatives of enterprise owners, workers and the government, or two parties. Hence, a committee does not simply mean the integration of the financially-connected institutions but also includes representatives of workers and employers. If financial autonomy is practiced, all the committees should decide the personnel management of various institutions. If China chooses financial autonomy completely under government administration, it is undoubtedly important to include people from other sectors at least.

It is imperative to strengthen management of the social security fund and perfect regulations.

It is of great importance to strengthen the management and use of the fund, which is closely related to the guarantee of the essential living of the vast number of workers and the success or failure of the social security work. According to statistics by departments concerned, in 1991, 30.33 billion yuan was collected for the old-age insurance fund and unemployment insurance fund while 24.988 billion yuan was spent. In recent years, social security managing institutions in various places formulated regulations on finance, accounting and statistics and some provinces set up internal auditing systems. Some departments also worked out corresponding nationwide working rules on booking, statistics and fund management. Nevertheless, there are still striking problems in these respects. First, there are cases of embezzlement. Second, there are serious wastes because of over-spending. Third, the problem of the value increment of the fund is not yet resolved. Now that China has decided to adopt the method of partial accumulation of the old-age insurance fund, the problem to keep or increase the value of the fund has become all the more outstanding. Hence, it is necessary to take the management and operation of the fund as the key to social security reform.

To perfect the fund managing system and change the situation without separating the government, institutions and enterprises. The business operating institutions should maintain relative independence besides receiving policy guidance and administrative supervision from competent departments.

To strengthen financial management. The business institutions must work out annual budget and final accounts of the revenue, expenditure and balance of the fund, and report to the people's congress at the same level after they are verified by the financial department, then report them to the province or state financial department and competent department in charge of social security.

To strengthen supervision and examination of the fund. It is important to form fund review and supervision committees made up of people from the audit, supervision, structure reform, trade union, finance and social security departments and representatives from enterprises, experts and scholars. The committee will hear reports by social security institutions and financial departments on the revenue and expenditure and collection, use and value increment of the fund. The result of the review will be reported to the government and the standing committee of the people's congress.

To attach importance to upgrading the level of the socialization of social security. First, it is necessary to expand coverage. Unemployment insurance coverage shall be expanded in the first place. In 1986, China started unemployment insurance. Its narrow coverage, only applicable to part of the workers (four categories of workers) in state-owned enterprises, does not conform to the demand of the deepening of the labor system reform, the transformation of enterprises' operational mechanism, the implementation of bankruptcy law and the rational circulation of labor. The development of a socialist market economy will inevitably expand social insurance coverage gradually to all workers in state-owned enterprises and workers in enterprises of other ownership. And then the coverage for old age, medical care and injury shall be gradually expanded for a steady establishment of a unified social security system. Second, it is necessary to upgrade management. China shall take, step by step, modern managing methods, provide socialized service, upgrade the management transparency and publish regularly relative data (including to government, enterprises and workers), so as to realize the goal of social security for enterprises and workers. Third, it is important to intensify the service of social security. The experience of socializing the distribution of retirement pensions shall be popularized. The intensification of social security work shall be linked with vocational service to provide opportunities of re-employment of the unemployed.

To intensify the legislation on social security. China shall formulate and promulgate as soon as possible laws and regulations on social security, perfect rules and regulations on its management and make clear definitions on the right, duty and obligation of each side so that everybody will have laws to abide by and rules to follow, to ensure a sound development of the social security cause along the track of legalization.

2. Management of the Rural Social Security Fund

The management of rural social security funds needs a fundamental policy with the emphasis on the increase of fund value.

There are three special points in China's rural social security system. First, its strongest point is that it does not have any burden, and without the question of reform, it will start anew from the beginning. Second, the greatest difficulty is the huge difference and unstable income. Third, the hardest thing for farmers to accept is pool raising of funds and on-the-spot collection and payment. Farmers do not like to accept the idea of giving money to others. Anyway, the pattern is from the basic method of Singapore's central public fund, that is, when a personal account is opened, subsidies will be given to them from collective funds and the interest and their savings will go to their accounts with high transparency. With the transparency, when farmers see how much they can get in the end (that is to say, there is a standard of payment according to predetermined rate of value increment), they will accept it. Later, an insurance mechanism, only as an auxiliary, is added to it, to achieve mutual adjustment between those of the same age, who may pass away at an early age or who may live a fairly long life. It is different from the Singapore approach, which means that there is nothing left if all the reserve is used up. Anyway, our total final sum to give is determined according to the total reserve.

How is the value of the sum of money reserved? The current approach is through the purchase of state bonds. The technical problem with buying bonds is already solved through consultations with the Ministry of Finance. Basically, local funds may go directly to the central finance, which issues to localities bonds that can be cashed but not circulated or transferred. Interest is generally paid on a monthly basis. The technical operational problems are already solved. The other part will be deposited in local banks. Various banks still pay high interest, whatever the central bank does to control it. The annual interest for savings may be as high as twelve percent, and carry no risks. The end-result will get better and better, along with the bank interest getting normalized on the market. China lacks funds, instead of possessing too much. Then how big will the reserve be? If a county needs 10 million yuan per year and there are 1,000 counties, it will amount to 10 billion yuan and the repayment in large quantities will be years later. It is a quite big reserve. Now it is fairly difficult to start the fund. Without the full mobilization of thousands of farmers by local governments, the all-round operation is impossible. So, the localities should be given the benefits. That is why it is explicitly explained that the right to use the fund is in the hand of the localities. The only condition is that the value is to be reserved with the interest increase according to the rules. The fund cannot be used to make direct investment but can buy bonds issued by the localities, or be deposited in local banks, which pay interest. The fund will be managed by civil affairs administrations, but the localities have the right to use it. Naturally the localities will be content with this.

From a long-term point of view, there should be a basic national policy. In Japan, part of the social insurance fund is invested by the Investment Bureau of the Finance Ministry. In Singapore, the early central public fund was mainly used for infrastructure construction, and the interest rate was very low, slightly over two percent, lower than bank interest rate. They believed the investment could bring more job opportunities. When everyone's income was increased through economic development, the reserve capability would be enhanced. The security level was substantially upgraded in this way, rather than through a single interest rate. Generally speaking, the government gained, instead of losing, by making the investment to provide more job opportunities and increase revenues. The Chinese Government should have a corresponding policy on security affairs in rural areas. Now, most of the regions are not very enthusiastic about it. It is a matter of a thirty to forty billion yuan fund. If the localities are not enthusiastic, the central authorities have to manage it. If the central authorities do not have a macro policy and do not issue special bonds, people will buy bonds that are issued first and deposits will be made at the banks that offer higher interest rate. The central authorities should have a policy on such a large fund. The fund may be contracted to projects like the national highway and railway construction or the Three Gorges project, and will have returns in the future. The reason for the adherence to a low level of the total reserve of the fund is based on the fear that too big a reserve will put a heavier weight on reserving the value. How low should it be then? The Ministry of Civil Affairs has suggested that the lowest level be connected with the current social relief policy. This means that the poverty relief must be connected with the lowest level. The high level should be lower than the basic living standard in urban areas. The Ministry of Civil Affairs holds that after the establishment of a basic insurance system in rural areas, more encouragement should be focused on towns and villages, including local enterprises, to run their own supplementary security plans by relying on their own capability. The participants and money involved should be more than the basic insurance and higher than the urban ratio. The fund risk of the self-run part goes under their own responsibility, instead of that of the government. They may choose their own investments and insurance companies. The fund management is based on balanced budget at county level. A slogan for the farmers is: If it is yours, it is yours, no matter it is your county, town, village or yourself, and the return will be given to you according to the publicized rate.

3. Establishing an Advanced Social Security Information Network

One goal for the reform of China's social security system is to ensure that enterprises will hold the responsibility to provide social security benefits to their workers and retirees. Though the old-age pension and some other benefits may be an additional burden to enterprises, it is much easier to let an institution rather than a central social security organization provide the benefits to enterprises, because enterprises have kept a complete record, such as workers name lists and their wage data. It is necessary to set up a communication channel to ensure that the above information may be shared by the two sides when a central organization is to take the responsibility. The social security organization needs to know every worker's wage to ensure that enterprises pay the right amount in the first place, and secondly, to enable them to assess how much the worker may get for his old-age pension and his benefits when he or she retires.

Along with the complication of social security benefits, there are more and more benefits in different names. It needs all the more detailed record of all kinds of data. If it is only related to retirement pension, it will be enough for enterprises just to provide wage data. If it involves some short-term benefits, such as the need to pay medical care, there needs to be an exchange of information every month. If the monthly information is not guaranteed, social security agencies will not be able to obtain the latest information of the enterprise and the benefit is delayed in the end and the sick worker may be put in a very difficult plight.

In general, the communication between enterprises and social security agencies is done through the list of payments, which has every worker's name, wage and the fee paid by the enterprise. An enterprise and its employees pay the charge every month through a bank which deposits the payment to the agency account number at the bank and issues a receipt and the payment list to the enterprise as a certificate of its payment. If it is on a monthly basis, a receipt will be attached to the payment list. If it is on a quarterly, or biannual basis, there will be either four or just two receipts. The receipt and payment list are helpful and very effective, to some extent, to the financial scrutiny and in preventing errors and fraud.

In designing a computer program, one first has to decide what kind of information the program will keep, e.g., what you want the program to do for you. Once the decision is made, the programmer should decide accordingly what data to keep, in what way and how long they will be kept. The work must be done carefully and meticulously by professionals. Some of the data may not be of any use for the time being, but may come in handy in the future or at the time when workers retire. It is impossible to collect the data on a worker of his previous years at the time of his retirement. It is important to ensure that the data collected from the very beginning is accurate and needed. You may feel it is unnecessary to keep record of the wage and the payment, when you use a computer, because the payment is a certain fixed percentage of the wage. But in some social security plans, there is a maximum line, above which there is no charge. Now the payment record may enable you to determine benefits after one retires, it may not satisfy all your requests. Here is an example. Fifteen years later, a social security agency may decide to raise the maximum line, then there is the need to find out the actual wage of those workers whose wage exceeds the maximum line, in order to set a new maximum line. This example shows that if the wage record is not kept, you will not be able to get the information when you need it. Most social security organizations have two clear and interrelated systems, a hardware system with two software systems, the payment system and the benefit system. Perhaps there are also the financial management system and the data statistics system. Anyway, they are smaller systems than the payment and benefit systems, which are the two most important ones.

On the payment system. It needs two systems within the payment system, the enterprise system and workers system. Data on workers should be taken into consideration first. The basic data on each worker should be filed, so as to differentiate one from another. Of course, names, dates of birth and ID numbers are the best marks. There are many cases that more than two people share one name, and they are even born on the same date, because China has a huge population. Then, the ID number may be of use. But the ID number is a long figure with fifteen digits. Enterprises usually give their workers a short social security number. For an enterprise, this works, because it only cares about its employees. It will be a trouble for a social security agency because it has to keep all the data of thousands upon thousands of enterprises, and it is possible that workers may have the same number. So, his social security number and his enterprise number are needed to determine a worker's identification. How about a worker moving from one enterprise to another? Will his social security number be changed? There is no problem when an enterprise keeps records of its employees. It will be a hard problem if it is in line with the reform. The purpose of enterprises is to guarantee the circulation of labor force to the greatest extent. This will make the problem more striking. Therefore, the only way out is to use the ID number rather than social security number. One of the goals of a good system is to reduce the number of digits needed to be repeatedly recorded. The 15-digit ID number runs counter to it. As far as putting in the data is concerned, no matter on computer or by hand, the more the digits, the more likely are errors. What is the consequence when a number is filed wrong? The wage and payment of one worker is filed under the name of another. To avoid such errors, the system designers have to make painstaking efforts.

Secondarily, the wage records. Workers' wages must be recorded in great detail, so that they may be taken as the groundwork for their old-age pensions. In general, the charge rate for old-age pension is based on the average wage of the worker's years of employment or his or her employment over a period of time. So, it is necessary to keep records of data throughout his or her years of employment. Is it just to file the general wage and annual wage or every month's wage? The data will increase gradually. It is the need of computerized data for social security. It is larger than other computerized data systems. In actual operation, wages may be recorded respectively without indexing. It can be indexed at anytime because the computer program has the function. Thanks to the fast calculation ability of computers, a worker's monthly wage throughout his whole life may be indexed. It would be a very heavy workload if it were done by hand. So much data and such a long period to keep means that the computer must have a very big memory. Computerized payment systems may quite easily file all the individuals' accounts if necessary.

On enterprises data. There are mainly two categories of data for enterprises, financial and statistical. Financial data is about the actual payment that enterprises pay for their employees, to help social security agencies know which enterprise has already paid the right amount. If the enterprise has not paid, or has not paid in time, the agency may take proper compulsory action. The statistical data may help social security workers accurately assess social security plans and work out models, which should be based on the solid and accurate file data. It depends on the type of benefit system, or what kind of benefit is needed and sometimes it is necessary to keep data about whether the enterprise makes profits.

On benefit system, which is another large computer system. It keeps record of the details of paying old-age pensions and other benefits. Enterprises may acquire, through computers, wage data in the payment system, so that they are able to figure out the fee rate for old-age pensions. The benefit system may file the details of every old-age pension receiver, and is able to prepare necessary documents to help pay him or her the pension each month. If the pension is deposited in the retiree's bank account, the system can prepare a list that is provided to each bank every month. If it is paid by check, the system should be able to print a real check. The only thing the system is not able to do is to give cash to the retiree. The benefit system shows that one of the striking feature of a computer system is its ability to handle tremendous daily routine work with excellent accuracy.

图书在版编目(CIP)数据

中国的社会保障制度/高尚全,迟福林主编.
—北京:外文出版社,1994
(经济丛书)
ISBN 7 – 119 – 01733 – 0

Ⅰ.中… Ⅱ.①高… ②迟… Ⅲ.社会保障制度
—中国 Ⅳ.D632

中国版本图书馆 CIP 数据核字 (94) 第 14634 号

中国的社会保障制度

高尚全　迟福林主编

责任编辑　程钦华

*

©外文出版社

外文出版社出版

(中国北京百万庄路 24 号)

邮政编码 100037

北京外文印刷厂印刷

中国国际图书贸易总公司发行

(中国北京车公庄西路 35 号)

北京邮政信箱第 399 号　邮政编码 100044

1996 年(大 32 开)第一版

(英)

ISBN 7 – 119 – 01733 – 0 /F·29(外)

02100

4 – E – 2953P